Teaching Reading in Secondary Schools

Geoff Dean

David Fulton Publishers

London

David Fulton Publishers Ltd
Ormond House, 26–27 Boswell Street, London WC1N 3JD

First published in Great Britain by David Fulton Publishers 2000

Note: The right of Geoff Dean to be identified as the author of this work has been asserted by him in accordance with the Copyright, Designs and Patents Act 1988.

Copyright © Geoff Dean 2000

British Library Cataloguing in Publication Data

A catalogue record for this book is available from the British Library

ISBN 1–85346–661–1

Typeset by FSH Ltd London
Printed in Great Britain by The Cromwell Press Ltd, Trowbridge, Wilts.

Contents

'Born to Read'
Name of Literacy initiative in Newcastle-on-Tyne
distributing books to babies

With my love to Karen, who always supports my work, while reminding me
how intrusive it can be!

Chapter 1
The Problems of Reading in the Secondary School

Reading is the most heavily researched single area of the whole curriculum, and yet, paradoxically, it remains a field in which a good deal of fundamental work has yet to be approached, and one in which a great many teachers would claim to be almost wholly ignorant. If this is true of teachers at the primary level, where for many an understanding of reading was founded on a single lecture in a three year college course, how much more does it describe the position of teachers in secondary schools, who have generally had no training at all related to reading but nevertheless feel conscious that the ability to read fluently is the basis for most school learning, and one of the surest predictors of academic attainment. (Harrison and Gardner 1977)

Reading is not taught in most secondary schools in England. Considerable numbers of activities in connection with books and other sorts of texts take place in classrooms, but these are not usually directed towards the improvement and growth of pupils' reading, except in a very limited sense.

Having stated that problem, it is not my intention to offer radically new solutions to deal with it, although I hope that I can draw together different strands of thinking on this topic capable of challenging much current practice. The authoritative sounding title of this book is intended to provoke interest in and to give greater prominence to an insupportable situation – the lack of teaching of reading – which has existed for too long in most secondary schools and urgently needs addressing. I want to describe a picture, currently familiar to most teachers of English and becoming increasingly important to teachers of other subjects, especially those who are seeking active ways of improving the learning of their pupils through greater attention to the language in which it is framed.

I believe that enormous numbers of secondary teachers instinctively realise that something has to be done about making a greater impact on and improving the reading and writing attainment of their pupils. Many are already attempting a variety of strategies. Yet most teachers – including English teachers – of pupils aged between 11 and 16 years know far too little about reading. Nothing was provided in their training or teaching experience to inform them of the details of teaching reading, or even to provide a background theory of reading. Something has to be done to inform teachers about reading, and reading must be taught.

Definitions of reading

Reading is a huge topic, potentially beset with myriad difficulties not easily addressed in a book of this length. Brindley (1994) in her introduction to the 'Reading' section of *Teaching English* offers a helpful starting point:

> Reading is a complex area. We can use the term to mean the process itself, or a response to literary text. It can mean the retrieval of information in a non-literary text, or take on wider meanings like 'reading the situation'. Reading is not confined to print in a book. It is central to the debate about meaning and the construction of the reader. It is linked to issues of standards in education, and to one of the functions of education itself – the production of a literate society.

This is a relatively focused view of reading. Andersen *et al.* (1985) provide a broader view of the same territory:

> The majority of scholars in the field now agree on the nature of reading: Reading is the process of constructing meaning from written texts. It is a complex skill requiring the coordination of a number of interrelated sources of information.
>
> Reading can be compared to the performance of a symphony orchestra. This analogy illustrates three points. First, like the performance of a symphony, reading is a holistic act. In other words, while reading can be analyzed into subskills such as discriminating letters and identifying words, performing the subskills one at a time does not constitute reading. Reading can be said to take place only when the parts are put together in a smooth integrated performance. Second, success in reading comes from practice over long periods of time, like skill in playing musical instruments. Indeed, it is a lifelong endeavor. Third, as with a musical score, there may be more than one interpretation of a text. The interpretation depends on the background of the reader, the purpose for reading, and the context in which the reading occurs.

There are other, more diffuse and yet equally important descriptions of the process, such as 'reading' moving and still visual images. A much wider concept, proposed by Paulo Freire, involves a sense of 'reading the world', but for the time being it will be more useful not to wander too far away from the descriptions offered above.

In the secondary school responsibility for reading is usually, but not exclusively, situated within the work of the subject known as 'English'. But reading takes place in so many contexts and for so many purposes across all schools that it can mean wholly different things in different circumstances. The problem with reading is that it is not a specific quantifiable act, or a collection of such acts, but the amalgam of a whole set of cultural practices. It can range from very deliberate and focused decoding of specific symbols to the seeking of generalised, overall impressions about the broadest topics. Pin down one part of reading, and another, related, aspect wriggles away. Massive amounts of research time and writing have been devoted to exploring the nature of reading; conferences are devoted to it; everybody concerned with education is agreed that reading competence is the really necessary prerequisite for academic success; but ask most teachers in the secondary school – particularly teachers of English – how they teach reading and a common answer is likely to be a shrug and a blank look.

Yet the one feature about reading on which all contemporary commentators and researchers seem to agree is that it should be an active, meaning-making enterprise, most often undertaken with a clear purpose, whatever the context.

The intention of this book is:

- to help teachers ask some fundamental questions about reading;
- to reconsider how they can improve the quality of meaning-making engagements their pupils make with texts;
- to support the ways they might plan for that improvement;
- to enable pupils to make realistic appraisal of their own reading practices;
- to employ devices for tracking and articulating how pupils are progressing and growing as readers.

This book is mostly directed towards teachers of English, but many of its principles, recommendations and methods apply to all teachers who expect reading (and writing) to feature significantly in the study of their subjects. Twenty-five years after Ronald Arnold HMI wrote, on behalf of the Bullock Committee (DES 1975), 'Since reading is a major strategy for learning in virtually every aspect of education we believe it is the responsibility of every teacher to develop it', the current Labour government, through its Education Standards and Effectiveness Unit, has introduced a national agenda that expects all secondary schools to improve pupils' literacy abilities – including reading – to enhance ways of learning. The argument for this broader attention to literacy, beyond the English classroom is:

1. Pupils have to be introduced to texts in their school subjects.
2. Those texts embody the uniquely related discourses of the different subjects.
3. Teachers of those subjects should supply the necessary clues and codes to make the clearest meanings of those texts in the contexts they are presented.

This book, therefore, has much to say to teachers of all subjects.

Issues relating to English in the secondary curriculum

Although this book is mainly about reading, it is not possible to address reading in isolation in secondary schools without asking some serious background questions about the subject called 'English', and its changing relationship with other subjects of the secondary curriculum. Because of recent significant educational developments, most obviously seen in the foregrounding of notions of 'literacy', the nature and content of English in the secondary curriculum are no longer as clear and certain as they might once have seemed. Indeed, in 1988, Professor Henry Widdowson, a member of the Kingman Committee investigating the teaching of the English language, challenged his fellow committee members to address these matters before they were in a position to make any substantial recommendations:

> What English is on the curriculum *for*, is not really explored here with any rigour, but simply asserted in very general (and traditional) terms. When this point was raised in committee, it was decided that any more radical enquiry into the purposes of English would be a distraction. I believe, on the contrary, that it was central to the Committee's concerns. For only when English has been clearly defined as a subject in relation to such purposes, when the vague notion of 'mastery' is given more specific content, can a statement be logically made about the knowledge of language that is necessary to achieve the objectives of English as a subject.

Poulson (1998), writing about the English curriculum, states:

> Regardless of educational reforms, and greater control over what schools do, we appear to be no nearer to stating what English is than in 1987, when Henry Widdowson identified this as the central task in relation to the subject. The question has largely been ducked.

Those with any real interest in the subject have to be prepared to ask some difficult but very straightforward questions as part of a necessary process of repositioning 'English' in a changing educational context. These should include the following:

- What is the subject known as 'English'?
- What are we teaching 'English' for?
- What is meant by teaching and learning in 'English'?
- What is meant by 'progression and growth' in 'English'?
- Who should decide what is contained in 'English'?
- What does 'English' have to do with 'literacy'?
- For which areas of 'literacy' should teachers of 'English' principally take responsibility?

These important and legitimate enquiries are increasingly being made by teachers in English departments and their school senior managers, because they realise that coherent and worthwhile progress in pupils' overall literacy attainment cannot be made without having attempted to answer them.

So why should the present be regarded as the proper occasion to examine the subject in this way? Frankly, this reappraisal is long overdue; such an examination should have been conducted at a much earlier period, but a number of distracting other agendas were forced on the subject and sapped its energies from the early 1980s. Nevertheless, the sorts of developing situations listed below have added extra urgency to the asking of these questions:

1. Teachers of English have just received the *second revision* of a National Curriculum, originally introduced a mere decade ago; this revision has been less politically motivated than previous versions, but is still subject to a variety of pressures and assumptions deserving of careful analysis by all who have to implement and work within the statutory orders of the subject.
2. Most primary schools in England, during the 1998/99 academic year, adopted the National Literacy Strategy, either whole or in part. The Strategy sets out language-based objectives to guide a more common programme of language and literacy studies for pupils in infant and junior classes across the country and has been introduced to raise expectations about pupil attainment. The impact of such a new, demanding and detailed programme of studies is bound to have increasing effect on the ways language and literacy courses in English will be taught in Key Stage 3 in every secondary school during the few years after its original implementation.
3. Examination syllabuses have been gradually evolving and changing at GCSE and A level to accommodate new theoretical influences and demands on the subject; A level assessment criteria, particularly, reflect the ways that 'critical theory' has begun to impinge on literary study in university literature courses, and are expected to align sixth form studies more closely with those in tertiary education.
4. A greater receptivity to 'reader response' theories – recognising that pupils bring a huge variety of different reading biographies to their school reading practices – has caused many teachers to reconsider their approaches to reading and obliged them to ask again what 'reading' might mean in the context of their departmental schemes of work.
5. Rapidly changing and growing technologies – including the implications of digitalisation and increasing technological textual overlaps and their growing widespread use – are causing new questions to be raised about the definition, use and study of 'texts'; it is no simple matter to decide what is meant by being 'literate' at the beginning of the twenty-first century; former notions of 'reading' and 'writing', under threat in relation to technological change, are subject to new interpretations (e.g. can one 'write' with a video

camera? How much 'writing' is taking place in editing information from the internet? Is watching a section of a film on DVD disc, in preparation for editing the order of the scenes, a 'reading' act?).

6. Formerly 'secure' theories relating to the rules and knowledge of language in texts studied in school have been challenged by a growing recognition of differing social contexts causing a variety of 'frameworks' for language deployment; 'genre theory' has meant the development of a new 'knowledge about language' (QCA's 1999 publication acknowledges the changing nature of this particular debate, referring back to its previous, quite different, publication distributed a whole year earlier!).

7. Teachers of English encounter huge difficulties, in the face of the sheer mass of available textual materials, deciding exactly what to introduce and study with their pupils in the classroom; they are even undecided about the nature of the literary works to deploy. An explosion of televisual media, magazine publishing, publishing for children and young adults, electronic games and internet connected materials, and the inexorable marketing of sport, fashion, media, food, drink etc., are causing departments to ask Which are the essential texts to include in our reading programmes?

8. Teachers of English share an intuitive sense that the current assessment procedures in their subject are inadequate and unhelpful; too little is sought and discovered about the ways pupils grow and progress as language users, especially for those in Key Stage 3, and that which qualifies for reporting purposes is too general.

Any one of these situations in isolation should give sufficient reason to question our former understandings about English; regarded collectively, they offer an overwhelming case for reconsideration of the subject. A government committed to reducing teacher bureaucracy and teacher stress was unlikely, however, to question the complete nature of a subject designated 'core' in the National Curriculum, but it was a lost opportunity, during the period of curriculum review in 1998/99, not to acknowledge that considerable changes are affecting English. It will therefore be wholly incumbent on English departments themselves to undertake this discussion of their own volition, if they are to maintain their work in language and literacy learning contexts which recognise the wholesale changes continuing to impact on the boundaries and definitions of the subject.

Implicit in the broad discussions which English departments should generate will inevitably be specific issues relating to reading and how that process should be described, approached, supported, taught, learned, resourced and assessed in the future. Confidence of and knowledge about reading in secondary schools have to be improved for staff in all departments, and those improvements are likely to be accelerated and more substantially based if the teachers of English themselves have agreed on their part in a whole-school undertaking. Secondary teachers should not complain about their pupils' reading deficiencies without themselves having a working knowledge of theories of reading (and writing) capable of bringing about change and progress.

Reading practices in secondary schools

In raising these issues, I do not want to give the impression that reading has been neglected by English teachers in secondary schools. Such a claim would be patently untrue and a gross misrepresentation of the hard work of many staff. English departments continually worry about how best to provide worthwhile reading experiences for their classes. They are always concerned about the obvious differences in reading attainment of pupils and make real attempts to redress them; they do their utmost to enable the least able to gain some success while continuing to challenge the more able. They constantly provide opportunities for pupils to become more interested in reading and many departments have set up a wide range of supportive activities for this very purpose.

Yet, despite these efforts, English teachers have rarely agreed with one another in their departments about what 'reading' means. Where colleagues in a department might have agreed a definition for their own purposes, it has not been shared or compared with definitions of other groups of teachers in their own and other schools. A serious questioning of the different encultured views of reading has not been undertaken on any real scale. At its simplest, most departments have not established for themselves what the desirable or necessary qualities of a 'reader' ought to be, and, therefore, reading programmes more specifically designed to promote those outcomes are not planned. Teachers have not had available, or been aware of, relevant and helpful materials or 'models' of assessment, to enable careful and discriminating tracking of 'reading' through progressive stages of growth. A Head of English quite recently described a three level assessment structure he used with his pupils:

- could they begin to read (by which he meant 'decode') the letters?
- could they make reasonable sense / make any meaning from the text?
- could they 'read between the lines'?

Nobody, by his own admission, had discussed with him the enormity of this topic during his professional career. Yet he encouraged his pupils to bring reading books to lessons, and they responded well. The classroom atmosphere and ethos were properly prepared for learning more about reading in all lessons in his department, but any potential teaching of reading stopped at that point, quite simply, because of teacher ignorance.

In all secondary English classrooms enormous numbers of activities related to certain sorts of texts are planned and take place every school day. These activities are mostly concerned with straightforward matters pupils are expected to find out about the text: considerations of character, plot, structure, setting, theme, occasionally language, and – very often – the social issues the text might raise. They tend to be practical activities, likely to help young people answer certain sorts of comprehension questions and prepare them for writing essays for examination purposes on their responses to the text (Poulson 1998) but there is no *teaching* about how a pupil might improve as a reader.

> There was an emphasis on how texts work; how language is used to communicate ideas; how authors create particular effects, or draw a reader into a story or a point of view; how a writer could reveal information to or withhold it from a reader. There was also emphasis on the content of novels, stories, plays and poems with, for example, discussion of issues presented in a text. Although literature, or rather texts, was the primary focus of content in English, some teaching about language also featured in classrooms.

A purpose of this book is to challenge much current practice in the teaching of English. It is unlikely to be a popular theme, but it is a topic that has to be reconsidered. I have become increasingly concerned as a teacher, local authority adviser, an OFSTED inspector and a parent that secondary schools are unable to articulate how a pupil might have made real progress as a reader particularly from Year 7 to Year 9. I have sat through too many lessons where pupils have been asked to undertake low-level activities designed to give them the simplest purchase on a text. Too regularly the reason for this work is unclear, and wholly unrelated to the reading backgrounds or life experiences of the children in the room. It often involves relegating vivid passages of language to the most threadbare starting points for superficial study. I have observed countless library lessons where many pupils fill in spaces of time, from 20 minutes to a whole hour, idly dipping in and out of reading books ('no non-fiction, remember!'), to little purpose. I have seen too many pupils, often boys, who begin to show a faint interest in a text, not supported to the next stage of insight or independent engagement. I have talked with large numbers of young people who do not know why they are expected to involve themselves in the 'reading' procedures going on around them. I have discussed with a wide range of pupils, during a research project exploring provision for pupils of more able linguistic attainment, the lack of challenge or development their schools fail to provide. My own children have spent far too long on undemanding novels in school, expected to attend to, at best, the most peripheral ideas related to those texts. They were never given reasons why those texts had been chosen for them, nor were they challenged as growing readers through the increasing engagements with the texts they had been given. Neither child grew as a reader in the school context, and they were not alone.

Problems of learning in language, especially learning reading

There are a number of reasons why the *teaching* of reading has not been central in the work of English departments, but only two will be explored here. Because

English, as a school subject in England, is not constituted as a body of knowledge but regarded more as a 'series of engagements', little theoretical underpinning has been promoted of what ought to take place in classrooms. A large body of theoretical writing about how children most effectively learn language and learn through language has been published, mostly from other parts of the world, but it has made only minimal impact on classrooms where English is taught in England (Peim 1999):

> There is little tradition of cultivating theoretical knowledge as a means for rethinking everyday classroom practices. Theories, debates and new practices... have drifted in and out of the subject, without deeply affecting its 'constitutional' habits.

Peter Traves, formerly LEA adviser, now head-teacher, recently claimed in a talk about secondary literacy, 'Teachers have been spoiled by too little theory!' – a view I readily endorse.

The consequence is that most new English teachers emerge from their training and take up teaching in their own classrooms in much the same manner as their teachers would have worked when they were themselves pupils. There has traditionally been too little emphasis on *learning* in the subject. Davies recalls the position of English teachers before the National Curriculum required a greater accountability in regard to their work:

> English teachers have often tended to be quite unfocused in the way they define their aims. That is to say, they often view what goes on in their classrooms in a very inclusive way, so that everything that happens in a lesson is counted as contributing to students' learning.

He makes the reasonable conclusion that 'if learning is in everything then it might sometimes be difficult to know whether it happened'.

A recent reviewer in the *TES* (Barton 1999) made the following claim of two newly published books about English:

> They focus on teaching, which at the end of the 20th century, isn't the real issue. The issue is learning. And the correlation between teaching and learning isn't always as inevitable as we might hope. Learning needs to be at the heart of the English agenda because teaching follows from it. Without a clear framework for the way children acquire and then develop language, for the way reading and writing skills develop, teachers can get locked into approaches that are ineffective.

Without an emphasis on learning, English teachers have explored only minimally what might be meant by progression in their work. The teaching has not been related sufficiently closely to bringing about possible known, planned outcomes. A lot of effort is regularly put into the planning of reading activities;

too little attention has been paid to the likely effectiveness of those activities, and virtually no time at all given to discovering if reading development has taken place.

Extraordinarily, there is no widespread agreement among English teachers about the nature of how pupils learn language, and guiding statements relating to the planning of learning in the subject are rare. The Language in the National Curriculum (LINC) project, set up as a result of the Kingman Report (1988), proposed the following underpinning theories about language, from which learning approaches can be extrapolated:

1. As humans we use language primarily for social reasons, and for a multiplicity of purposes.
2. Language is dynamic. It varies from one context to another and from one set of users to another. Language also changes over time.
3. Language embodies social and cultural values and also carries meanings related to each user's unique identity.
4. Language reveals and conceals much about human relationships. There are intimate connections, for example, between language and social power, language and culture, and language and gender.
5. Language is a system and is systematically organised.
6. Meanings created in and through language can constrain us as well as liberate us. Language users must constantly negotiate and renegotiate meanings.

The *First Steps* research programme (Rees 1994), developed by teachers and academics over a period of five years through the Education Department of Western Australia, links language assessment with teaching and learning. It determined the following theoretical assumptions, as the starting point for language-based activities and assessment:

• Language learning takes place through interactions in meaningful events, rather than through isolated language activities.
• Language is seen as holistic; that is each mode of language supports and enhances overall language development.
• Language develops in relation to the context in which it is used; that is, it develops according to the situation, the topic under discussion, and the relationship between the participants.
• Language develops through the active engagement of the learners.
• Language develops through interaction and the joint construction of meaning in a range of contexts.
• Language learning can be enhanced by learners monitoring their own progress.
• The way in which children begin to make sense of the world is constructed through the language they use and reflects cultural understandings and values.

An English department adopting a set of underpinning theories, such as those above, would enable its teachers to establish a more clearly defined 'centre' to their work. An English team committed to a view about how pupils learn language ought to be constantly referring back to that set of first principles in all its planning, teaching and assessment procedures. That theory would not become a neglected set of rhetorical ideas gathering dust on a shelf, but have an existence utterly intrinsic to the work of the department guiding a consistently shared approach.

Lack of attention to learning in English has been attributed to the 'non-linear' nature of language acquisition. Most teachers of English claim that learning in language, unlike that, for instance, in mathematics, is not 'sequential'; the stages do not rely wholly on each other in an orderly, hierarchical manner. Learning in language is likely to take place over time, through a number of familiarising engagements across a range of contexts, with individuals moving forwards in spurts and bursts. This model of learning, based closely on that proposed by Jerome Bruner, is usually depicted as a 'spiral'. The thinking most often articulated in relation to it is that if pupils pass through a sufficient number of similar language and textual experiences, they will eventually pick up more secure understanding of them at points commensurate with their academic development. So a pupil's supposed reading growth could possibly be evidenced by entries in a reading log, tracing reading of gradually more 'sophisticated' texts. Yet it would be unlikely that those texts had been chosen for any particular developmental reading qualities; they were deemed more difficult, perhaps because certain writers are thought to present more 'challenging' reads, although the actual criteria of supposed difficulty do not rely on any scale.

This approach means that the ultimate learning intentions of those textual engagements can easily be overlooked in the effort of providing a range of interesting activities, and, unless the separate 'parts' of the learning are being closely monitored, they are not easy to track over time.

The second set of assumptions obstructing developing ideas of 'learning' in English have to do with thinking of learning in 'language' *en bloc*. Whilereading, writing, speaking and listening cannot successfully be taught in isolation, the four separate elements cannot always be given satisfactory attention unless the learning intentions of each have been identified at an early planning stage. While learning in language and literacy necessitates reading, writing, speaking, and listening being almost seamlessly integrated, learning in reading, learning in writing, learning in speaking and learning in listening really ought to be approached in four quite deliberate and separate ways. Yet this is not the way that language learning is usually approached or planned in English; a broad attention is usually given to broader subject issues. Specific learning in reading has, therefore, been largely neglected.

The wording of the National Curriculum has also not supported specific aspects of the teaching of reading. While urging teachers to regard reading, writing, speaking and listening as separate elements, worthy of equal amounts of teaching time (properly updating a view not common in the mid-1980s), the National Curriculum statutory orders do not then go on to emphasise key learning points in the separate elements. The section on reading in Key Stages 3 and 4 in *English in the National Curriculum* (DFE 1995) continually refers to 'opportunities' and pupils being 'encouraged' in regard to textual encounters; sometimes 'given access to'. Pupils should 'extend' their 'ideas', 'reflect on' a writer's 'presentation of ideas', or 'compare and synthesise information' in relation to factual and informative texts. They should be 'taught' to 'extract meaning', 'analyse' and even 'analyse and engage with', but nowhere is there any sort of reference to *learning*. It would be naïve of me not to realise that learning is supposed to follow from teaching, but this assumption has been too easily made in the past, without detailed assessment follow-through to check how much learning has actually taken place. I also contend that some of the specific skills pupils are expected to develop, as outlined in the National Curriculum, often in literary contexts, are not necessarily the same as those which might be regarded as 'learning to read' in much broader terms for wider contexts across the curriculum.

Teaching of reading in the secondary school

Every school should work out a clear view about the nature, teaching, learning outcomes, resourcing and assessment of reading, to be shared and understood by all their teachers. Yet, traditionally in secondary schools, the business of reading has been regarded as the province of the English department and it is most unusual to find teachers from other disciplines actively concerning themselves with its development. Unfortunately, the reality is that very few teachers – of English or any other subject – have well-developed ideas about reading and, therefore, a collaborative guiding sense of reading, including how to teach it, has neither been regarded as a necessity nor been developed in most schools.

The second reason why the teaching of reading has not become a customary part of the English programme in the secondary school curriculum is because almost no teachers know enough about it. Mention 'teaching' of reading, and English teachers raise their arms, shrug in a despairing manner, and explain that, 'nobody in this department has ever been taught how to teach it'. If teachers of English have only the most cursory knowledge of teaching of reading, their colleagues in other subjects are unlikely to have any at all.

Indeed, until recently there was an established view in secondary schools that the teaching of reading was a task exclusively reserved for teachers in primary education. Secondary teachers blamed the teachers in schools attended by their pupils before the age of 11 for any problems about reading. A few teachers supporting children with special needs might admit to teaching a limited form of reading, but few others played an active part in the process. English teachers have begun to realise that they might be responsible for the continuing development of this linguistic element, but little has been done to make it a reality. Virtually all teachers of other subjects have never considered the view that if they place texts before their pupils they really ought to provide those pupils with the most effective means of making the fullest meaning from them.

There is, however, a strong likelihood that this unsatisfactory situation is about to improve. In the summer term of 1999, a quarter of a century after publication of the Bullock report expectations, the government invited all secondary schools to attend 'literacy conferences' led by their local authority advisers, to consider this very issue. As part of the National Literacy Strategy, teachers in secondary schools are obliged – for the first time – to realise that they are in a position to improve their pupils' reading attainment. Whatever the reading backgrounds of their pupils prior to transfer to secondary school, teachers are no longer allowed to adopt a retrospective attitude of blame. They are expected to act, to make good any reading shortfall of the pupils in their school. The National Literacy Strategy document (Literacy Taskforce 1997) – rather confusingly – states:

> 112. Every secondary school should specialise in literacy and set targets for improvement in English (*sic*). Similarly, every teacher should contribute to promoting it. The principles for the management of literacy set out earlier apply as much to secondary schools as to primary schools. In shaping their plans it is essential that secondary schools do not see work on reading and writing as exclusively the province of a few teachers in the English and learning support departments.

The first sentence of this extract illustrates a lack of clarity in the relationship between literacy and English, which continues to bedevil real development.

Traditionally, in England and Wales, a great deal of energy has been given to ensuring that children aged 4 or 5 years, entering school, begin reading as soon as possible. The single most important pursuit in infants' schools is that of initial literacy, which has usually meant more attention being given to reading than writing. Unfortunately, this same commitment has rarely been sustained into Key Stage 2, where insufficient numbers of pupils fail to continue to make reading progress. After passing through the initial decoding stage, the majority of pupils are not exposed to a continuing progressive programme of reading development. These pupils have been regularly encouraged to read independently; to be read to by teachers and other adults and set tasks in which reading plays a real part, but they have not been tutored in mastering the increasing range of skills and ways of making meaning from the sorts of texts which their more demanding learning programme requires. Not surprisingly, OFSTED and other monitoring agencies have detected a growing 'tail' of pupil underachievement developing in Key Stage 2. Unfortunately, the longer many pupils stay in school, the further behind they fall. This situation is especially true for too many boys.

Most children aged 11 move to secondary schools where they encounter an enormous range of texts, many quite different from those encountered in their primary background. Yet only a handful of schools have devoted any time to exploring what 'reading' might mean for pupils in their new setting, and few have any sense that the process of 'reading' actually changes from text to text. Even teachers of English, who might be expected to have the most obvious concern with textual materials and literacy understanding, albeit of a 'literary' nature, have not been clear about their own textual responsibilities. As more and more National Curriculum directives – not always with strictly educational intentions – have been thrust on them, teachers were distracted from considering carefully what the most important priorities in their work might be. Ten years after the Cox Committee attempted to assist teachers of English in a clearer understanding of the textual range they could be expected to cover, English departments have lost the thread of the discussion the original National Curriculum documentation was written to promote. As a result of incessant revisions and extra requirements, very few English teams have, subsequently, made the time or found proper opportunities to step back from their day-to-day work to ask more fundamental questions about the nature of the material they should be incorporating into their programmes of study. The contribution each sort of text might make to wider reading achievement has also been neglected.

Paucity of liaison dialogue between feeder primary schools and the receiving secondary school has prevented consistent approaches to reading being developed at each stage of the pupil's school experience. Not much has changed since the Bullock Report (DES 1974) asserted:

> We also suggested that liaison between primary and secondary school should be so close as to allow the child to go on perceiving English as a continuous experience without sharp breaks. Our visits to schools led us to conclude that this is all too rarely achieved.

Models and theories of reading

Until the introduction of the National Literacy Strategy many teachers of the youngest children, when asked how they *teach* reading, might have referred to 'phonics', or 'contexts', or 'reading schemes', not themselves actually ways of teaching, but resources or emphases supporting the process. There was no common notion about the teaching of reading from school to school. It was possible to visit primary schools where the teaching of reading was not even consistent from Key Stage 1 to Key Stage 2. In those circumstances, the articulation of reading practices shared with secondary schools was wholly remote. The National Literacy Strategy *Framework* document (DfEE 1998), which accompanied the implementation of the National Literacy Strategy in the summer of 1998, introduced the Searchlights model of reading (see Figure 1.1). This model of reading (and writing) draws together a range of strategies 'each of which sheds light on the text', and is likely to become the predominant model.

The Searchlights model, in turn, is drawn from the extensive findings of researchers such as Marilyn Jager Adams and her team (Adams 1990), and a host of other materials, most notably *The Reading Book* (Barrs and Thomas 1991). The consistent message from these publications stresses that the process of reading is dependent on a number of factors, all working together. Reading is *not* just the decoding of black marks. Reading is *not* an activity that can just happen if children are exposed to lots of rich resources. The reader has to call on a number of areas of previous knowledge to 'get underway' as a reader. Reading with any sort of fluency means that the reader has to call on an array of linguistic principles to enable the text to have any sort of sense.

The National Literacy Strategy, then, promotes a view of reading built on the combined use of three forms of pupil knowledge:

1. **semantic knowledge** (what the text means/what kind of text), which equates with the Searchlights model's 'knowledge of context';
2. **syntactic knowledge** (the ways the words work together/what sorts of words), which equates with 'grammatical knowledge'; and
3. **grapho-phonological knowledge** (decoding and calling on sounds to represent the letter symbols), which equates with 'phonics – sounds and spelling' and 'word recognition and graphic knowledge'.

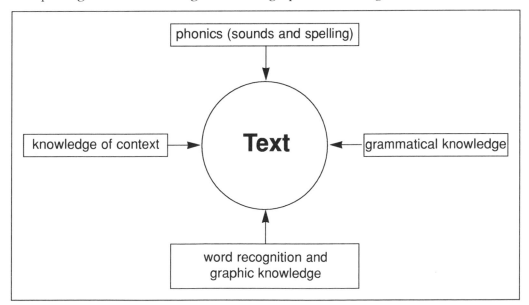

Figure 1.1 The NLS 'Searchlights' model of reading

The expectation of the Strategy is that each of these three areas of knowledge must be taught in a balanced programme to primary children, through the objectives in the **text level** (semantic), **sentence level** (syntactic) and **word level** (grapho-phonological) columns as specified in the *Framework for Teaching*. From September 1999, pupils arriving in secondary schools will be more familiar with this structure, year on year, as they experience more Literacy Hours. It will make considerable sense for teachers in secondary schools to adopt the approach outlined above as a starting point for their own teaching of reading. The possibilities will be explored later in this book.

The relationship between reading and writing

Another area of language learning made clearer and more explicit by the National Literacy Strategy is the relationship between reading and writing. Teachers and pupils in secondary schools will have to realise, as those in primary schools are discovering, that reading and writing are inextricably linked. Indeed, they can be regarded as much the same activity, but from different directions.

Authors produce texts for particular purposes, for intended audiences, within broadly understood rules relating to genre or text type. Writers learn to compose a greater variety of texts by becoming increasingly familiar, through reading and study, with a range of different texts in different contexts. Readers seek the purposes of texts, or choose them because they are already aware of what they are about; they check the ways in which the audience is being addressed, and operate their knowledge of genres and text types, to determine the proximity of the text to their original preconceptions. In school, we can help many young people to become more confident and competent readers and writers by bringing the two processes much more closely together.

Assessment

Finally, in this section, it is necessary to explore briefly some of the ways in which the limited range and nature of assessment have inhibited teaching and learning of reading. Because little theory underpins reading in secondary schools, insufficient attention is given to assessing pupils' progression as readers. Beyond the English department there is usually no record or sense of each pupil as a reader apart from the most superficial 'reading test score'. Considerable numbers of secondary schools test their pupils on entry, but the reliability and comprehensiveness of those tests are often compromised by the conflicting pressures of conducting and processing them as quickly as possible. Put simply, if a school administers a test taking only 30 minutes and expects from it an unexplained numerical outcome, it will not learn much about the reading attainment of its pupils. Teachers with responsibility for these tests are not usually able to explain exactly what the test was designed to demonstrate! They are also often unaware that many tests are over 50 years old, and that some references made in them are unfamiliar to today's pupils (particularly those from non-English speaking ethnic backgrounds). They rarely ever offer any indication of the reading potential of pupils, given proper support, which is just as important to know.

Even within English departments, there is sparse evidence of reading attainment beyond records of texts read in school or borrowed from the library. Sometimes 'comprehension' exercises are employed to discover how pupils question texts, and many teachers, through class discussion, gauge how their pupils approach textual experiences. Departments might maintain tick boxes and reading records, quite often related to 'Level descriptions' of the National Curriculum, but these are unlikely to contribute much to reading progress, if what is meant by reading progress has not already been established. The essential component of pupils' monitoring of their own progress is not regularly deployed, and too many young people are unable to describe how well they might be developing as readers, or how to reflect on their reading practices.

Conclusion

Schools have so many demanding requirements to satisfy these days that it is difficult to know which priorities have to be responded to and met first. There is little dispute, however, that if pupils are not making satisfactory progress in reading, everything else concerned with learning and attainment in the school will suffer. Even in schools where pupils achieve good results relative to national expectations, there is likely to be potential for further development leading to greater institutional success if reading is given more attention. This is not a matter of concern solely in to areas of social deprivation or under-achievement.

Some schools have written policies in the past few years, describing their attitude and approach to reading, believing that they have 'cracked' the problem. Unfortunately, failing to implement those intentions fully, or not monitoring their developments, is unlikely to lead to real improvement. Reading policies should be evident through all the school's operations, such as: departmental awareness and monitoring; staff recruitment and induction; assessment and record-keeping; uses and development of the learning centre/ library; purchase, storage and availability of textual resources throughout the school, and the ways it plans for learning.

Chapter 2

Current Reading Practices in Secondary Schools

Readers are made, not born, and they are made or unmade largely at school
(West 1986)

Reading in the English Department – Key Stage 3

It would be most unusual to discover an English department not claiming to improve its pupils' reading somewhere in the documentation explaining its work. Yet a great many English departments have no written policy or outline plan designed to bring about that improvement. What exactly the department means by 'reading' (even the simple recognition that it is a complex process) has usually not been defined and shared by groups of English staff and detailed agreement about the topic has rarely been discussed. The notion of 'reading' mostly remains a rhetorical idea in secondary schools in England. Similarly, the ways in which 'readers' make progress or could develop are often assumed by teachers in each English department, but not articulated and shared by most teams. The devices and mechanisms employed to measure how well pupils can read, where they exist, are superficial, clumsy and limited.

The intrinsic relationship between reading and writing is not usually spelled out to the pupils. The resources designed to support and enhance reading practices have not been specifically selected for their capacities to highlight and promote particular skills or identified needs. The individual reading requirements and interests of the pupils are often not well enough known to their teachers, and pupils' individual reading 'backgrounds' and reading biographies have been insufficiently explored. Girls, on the whole, are generally perceived as being more 'comfortable' with books and, in the main, they settle to read silently (i.e. engaging unproblematically with texts) more readily than boys. English teachers try to ensure the study of a range of texts, to meet the requirements of the National Curriculum and because they want their pupils to encounter genuine variety, but the contents of that range have rarely been fully explored and few actual choices are made against defined guidelines.

Most English teachers asked to show evidence for each pupil's reading 'growth' through years 7, 8 and 9 might refer the questioner to a reading log, some examples of written 'responses' to texts and, possibly, scores from reading tests. These logs and responses, however, are not capable of offering more than a record of names of texts encountered, whilst the numerical scores yielded by the tests would be unable to point to how actual reading progress has been accomplished, or offer advice about what teachers should do to promote further growth for specific pupils. An interested and informed parent of a Year 9 pupil asking for the details of their child's reading progression through Key Stage 3 is unlikely to receive a very full answer at the majority of parents' curriculum evenings!

This wholly bleak representation of the situation in English classrooms is overstated, but firmly enough based on real experience to be worthy of attention. English departments differ from one another in many ways, but the differences in practice of departments which have developed sound and fully supportive attitudes to reading and those which have not are enormous. Teachers take their responsibilities about improving pupils' reading very seriously; it is after all supposedly one of the main features of the English curriculum: '...it is the particular responsibility of the English teacher to teach reading in and *for itself*' [author's italics] (Fleming and Stevens 1998) and '...the business of reading, one way or another, has been central to the practices and to the ideological structure of English since the subject began.' (Peim 1993)

English teachers enjoy reading. One of the main reasons that most teachers of English chose their particular career is because they experienced such pleasure from reading when themselves pupils. They realised at quite an early stage in their lives that reading was much more than merely passing through texts. They probably mostly read and studied fiction texts as pupils in their English lessons. They discovered for themselves, or were helped to find, a wide variety of fiction texts, and they worked out which ones they particularly enjoyed. They were encouraged, and found it relatively easy, to ask an increasing repertoire of questions about many features of the texts placed before them, and those questions gradually became the critical analysis material of their post-16 study years. They tuned into an interactive relationship with texts, which yielded enormous personal gratification and became a pastime in its own right, often involving engagements with considerable numbers of texts beyond the school or university curriculum. They talked enthusiastically with like-minded readers about new texts just read, and recommended titles of their particular favourites to friends. They learned to trust the judgements and recommendations of certain people, and to reject those of others. They acted, indeed, as readers. Reading is such a pleasurable experience for themselves that they have a driving urge to make it possible for the young people they teach to have access to similar delights. Not surprisingly, then, that a foremost aspiration of many teachers of English is for their pupils to 'read for enjoyment'.

The literary experiences and backgrounds of most children they teach, however, are different. Whilst plenty of teachers work alongside pupils who have positive and encouraging early experiences with books, there are just as many who teach classes filled with those whose reading histories have not been anything like as smooth or as naturally integrated into their lives as those of their teachers. Considerable numbers of these children (about 4.6 million, according to a *Guardian* survey in September 1999) were not read to regularly when much younger, they infrequently – if ever – visited libraries, and there were few books or other written textual materials in their homes as they grew. They were more accustomed to exploring their narrative adventures and tales in televisual and comic page forms. Their mums might read stories or magazines for their own pleasure, but most of the men in their lives read little beyond the sports pages of, usually, tabloid newspapers. They encountered few models of reading beyond the purely pragmatic; reading for pleasure did not feature as a commonplace activity in those surroundings.

The early reading stages for many of these children are not effortless paths leading quickly to independent success. They are likely to have been filled with false starts and impenetrable culs-de-sac. Whilst they might be able to attach sounds to symbols, making their way reasonably successfully through small-scale phonics-based work, the 'real' textual sustained reading material provided for them is not always able to furnish them with meanings or issues they can relate to their own lives or interests. They might find it impossible to 'hear' these texts, to pick up the nuances and intentions of the authors hidden in the patterns and rhythms, to realise that they have to call on other sorts of knowledge 'of the world' to bring the text under review fully into the open. They have probably not been helped to see that different sorts of texts call for different sorts of skills; indeed, that before some texts can make any sort of sense the reader has to be preparing for what it is likely to offer. In short, to be taking part in something called reading, readers need to know that they have to be intellectually very busy (Strang 1976).

> There are many misconceptions of reading. To some people, words are merely the supplement to pictures, an adjunct to television. To others, reading is a passive process – 'expecting the book to come to you,' as one student said. Many people have been persuaded that reading is synonymous with word calling; if you can pronounce the words correctly, you are reading – even though you have no idea what the author said.
>
> Reading is more than seeing words clearly, more than pronouncing printed words correctly, more than recognizing the meaning of isolated words.

Reading requires you to think, feel, and imagine. Effective reading is purposeful. The use one makes of reading largely determines what is read, why it is read and how it is read.

Huge numbers of pupils fail to understand the sorts of prerequisites outlined in the preceding paragraphs. As they grow older, passing through Key Stage 2, there is an educational expectation that they will use and become more comfortable with an increased variety of texts for a wider range of purposes. Pupils already lagging behind their more successful peers in meaning-making aptitude at the earliest stages encounter exponentially greater difficulties in catching up, with increasing frustration. Actually, they rarely catch up at all; if they are not already disheartened by their inability to 'tread water', they simply do not bother to engage with the textual material they encounter. The researcher Connie Juel (1988) discovered, in a longitudinal study of children in American schools in the 1980s, that those who struggle in the early stages soon decide that they neither like reading nor want to read. As our society ascribes such enormous kudos to reading ability, educational success is regularly measured in those terms. To be a 'good reader' is synonymous with 'doing well' at school. (How many headteachers of secondary schools define their annual intakes of pupils by their 'reading scores'?) Large numbers of pupils between the ages of 9 and 14 see themselves as poor readers – because of the difficulties they experience in textual encounters – and write themselves off as far as personal further educational advancement is concerned at that stage. Being assigned to lower sets in their secondary schools merely confirms, officially, the view they have formed of themselves. To make real educational progress pupils have to believe that their efforts are worthwhile; if they begin from a position of low self-esteem caused by poor reading achievement, they are unlikely to make any effort at all.

What, therefore, takes place in secondary schools that is designed to change and improve these matters?

Teachers of English give many opportunities for all their pupils to practise their reading. Because a large proportion of pupils do not read much beyond the school classroom, teachers try to make sure they have timetabled English opportunities to encounter textual material. 'Reading' is an important starting point for much of the English curriculum. Teachers plan work that will not only bring their pupils into contact with a broad range of texts, but is also intended to help them to discover real meaning in those texts. Teachers read with pupils, read to pupils, listen to pupils reading and encourage pupils to read by themselves. But they do not *teach* reading and, as a result, far too many pupils fail to make satisfactory progress in reading between the ages of 11 and 14. General reading underachievement is not really dealt with any more successfully in Key Stage 4. At least, during years 10 and 11 there are more specific literary textual activities to set before classes, demanded by the GCSE examination syllabuses. These rarely relate to or grow naturally from the school's or the

English department's own view of reading, because, as already pointed out, these mostly do not exist.

So what does reading usually mean in the Key Stage English 3 classroom?

The class reader

All English teachers provide reading lessons, and lessons in reading, for their pupils. In many schools this might be through the study of a **class text**: multiple copies of the same book (likely to be a work of prose narrative fiction), chosen to be read with everybody in one class. After some preliminaries ('Has anybody read this book?' 'Has anybody heard of this author?' etc.), the teacher starts the reading, and pupils are encouraged to read a paragraph each, or a page – or, in some circumstances, the teacher or a pupil reads the narrative, and pupils read the dialogue of individual characters, a bit like a play script. Ways of approaching the text will differ enormously. Few teachers will merely plough on through the text, checking occasionally that everybody understands the difficult words or stopping to set written exercises or an essay title to test comprehension. More often, teachers offer a contextual introduction to the book, pause frequently in the reading to engage pupils in wider discussion, sometimes devising 'projects' or group enterprises, at appropriate levels of attainment, to enable the text to have greater relevance for all the readers.

The problems with this very common way of bringing books and pupils together are obvious.

What criteria are being employed in the selection of the book to be shared?

Some of these criteria are:

1. Too often the book is chosen because 'it is there'. The English department store cupboard has a stock of available books, built up over previous years. Because the titles already belong to the department, it would be an awful waste not to read them! English teachers are always reluctant to throw away books, so the collections in some cupboards are really large.
    English stock cupboards are worthy of study in their own right. They reveal so much about a department, and are often the best starting point for a department asking some serious questions about itself:

*   'Whose stock cupboard is it?' Does it belong to current staff, or was it put together by a previous group of teachers? Does it represent the thinking of the Head of English, or is it a more democratic collection, to which other members of the department can lay claim? Have any of the contents been chosen by pupils? Should pupils be included in purchasing decisions?

- Does it 'belong' to an examination board? Has much of it been filled to meet the requirements of syllabuses?
- Does the stock offer clues about an unsure group of teachers, or a confident team, able to use a range of texts for exploratory purposes? (Degrees of uncertainty can often be detected in the number of textbooks still in use.)
- Which texts are currently at eye level? Which are on the top shelves, having been relegated in status?
- When were some of the piles of texts last distributed? Are there records of issue dates to monitor use?
- Are texts labelled on shelves merely by title, or are they categorised in any other way?

2. It might be that the text in question is the one always allocated to year 7, at that time, whatever the collective abilities or interests of each separate class from year to year. The worst situation observed was a term by term list of books allocated to classes setted by ability through Key Stage 3, still in operation five years after it was devised without having ever been evaluated. The books supposedly ranged from 'simple' readers to the more difficult. Only the most superficial criteria had been used to decide what constituted a 'simple' text. The assumptions about books and reading in this department were huge; the pupils hated the reading lessons.

3. Sometimes the book is chosen because it happens to a 'favourite' of the teacher. Books should, of course, be presented to pupils with enthusiasm and in the most attractive and invitational light, but reasons for choosing them need to be rather more substantial than this. A few personal choice texts are still being presented to pupils, without any further rationale, in what I think of as 'The Silver Sword Syndrome'.

4. Books are occasionally selected because the department takes seriously its responsibility to ensure that pupils encounter a range of texts from different genres. So the department might choose a mystery for one term, a science fiction text for another and an action adventure story for a third. This approach, however, does mean that separate, individual genres can only be visited very occasionally, and there is little opportunity for development of further knowledge or developed exploration of that genre over time. Once again, teacher choice plays a significant part on pupils' experience.

5. In a few extreme cases, books have been selected because their subject matter seems to 'fit' a theme, topic or project already decided. So *Kestrel for a Knave* has comments to make about 'families', or *The Red Pony* might be suitable for an animal project! I have seen *The Diary of Anne Frank*, *Fireweed* by Jill Paton Walsh and *War Boy* by Michael Foreman read simultaneously by three different ability sets – in apparently descending order of difficulty – by Year 8 groups all studying war. If only all the groups had access to all of them there might have been some worthwhile areas of comparison to conduct.

6. Departments might select the book in question because they have been recommended titles which 'worked well' with similar groups in other schools. While it can be helpful to learn about new texts through recommendation, there are many reasons why a book might be welcomed by the pupils in one classroom, but not prove to be as popular in another.

7. Increasingly, groups of teachers are selecting titles of books reviewed in magazines such as *Books for Keeps*, reading a single copy each independently and then comparing their opinions with colleagues before deciding about buying a set. This method of selection does, at least, involve staff in discussion about the reasons for studying texts. In a few rare cases, pupils are themselves being invited to suggest titles likely to be popular with their classmates. This procedure is more usual in schools where initiatives such as 'tracking' the Carnegie Award (later in this chapter) are becoming more commonplace.

Only rarely will a book be chosen because it has satisfied some predetermined principles, adopted by the department and playing a part in their theories of reading progression.

What proportion of the class is expected to enjoy or engage with the book?

Too often, there is an assumption by the English teacher that the pupils will enjoy the text chosen for them, and it is disappointing if there are signs of dissent. This text, the teacher reasons, has been around a long time and lots of pupils have enjoyed it; why then should pupils in this group find it unacceptable? Excuses are employed: it must be the fault of the pupils/ I have not given them sufficient help to engage fully with it/ these pupils are not very successful readers. Thus the text is thought to be more important than the reader.

Later in this book, I shall try to explore the sorts of qualities that might help teachers define readers. One of these characteristics is: 'a reader will be able to explain why a text has been rejected, unfinished'.

If the department had in place some principles about reading, and what it means to be a reader, the teachers would already have thought about the possibility of some pupils, quite reasonably, suggesting that they would not wish to read on much beyond the beginning of a particular text. This process of 'selection' – not rejection – is a vital part of learning to be a reader, and should be thought of as permissible by pupils.

It is also necessary for pupils to know why a text has been selected on their behalf. If it is agreed that 'language learning is enhanced by learners monitoring their own progress', it follows that pupils should develop a clear sense of how they respond to and form relationships with particular texts, or types of texts. It is the duty of the school to introduce new textual experiences to young people. Therefore, in exploring with a class why a book is regarded as a typical example of, for instance, what might be classified 'science fiction', the teacher is not only teaching attributes of that genre, but allowing the pupils to decide whether they are interested in that sort of textual material. And whether they would wish to encounter more like it.

For some pupils, reading aloud to their peers in a whole-class setting is a very intimidating and frightening prospect. Most English teachers are sensitive to this predicament, and usually invite only volunteers to read aloud; but there is an implied sense of failure in not being confident enough to volunteer. A few departments insist that all pupils should, at least, attempt to read aloud a few sentences from a text, and this causes disruptions in its flow. Many good readers can remember being totally bored waiting for less assured classmates to stumble through passages they did not understand, and for which they could draw on no recognisable context. I remember, as a pupil, always reading books in class at two points; one at the page I had reached at my own pace, while keeping a finger inserted in the page everybody was still hearing aloud, in case I was called on to 'carry on' reading or to answer a specific question.

It is important to consider the choice of text from the pupil's point of view. Which parts of the reading process are intended to be addressed through this particular experience? How is the chosen book meant to contribute to pupils' reading progression? These questions are explored in more detail later in this chapter.

The class reader has been a feature of English classrooms for almost as long as the subject has been taught, and many teachers would claim it has genuinely positive values. Firstly, it provides a way of ensuring that everybody in the class is reading. It is a shared vehicle, enabling teachers to tackle matters of textual knowledge in a coherent manner with large groups of pupils, and teachers can address identified problems for the majority of the class as they arise. It is a way of checking the reading-aloud fluency of pupils and their relative levels of comprehension at a shared degree of difficulty. It can assist class control considerably. Many teachers are often able to inject enormous energy and life into the reading, which can be enjoyed by everybody, capable of breaking through the resistance to reading felt by some pupils. Pupils regularly 'catch' an infectious enthusiasm from the teacher, and continue reading the text independently in their own time.

In their own book, Fleming and Stevens (1998) quote some of the interviews Calthorpe conducted for his work (1971), with readers who

... felt that the shared experience of reading a common book was something of great value to themselves and their classes. They regarded it as something quite different from the pleasure to be gained from individual reading and took the view that the feeling of sharing something worth while, the common sense of enjoyment, and the resulting sense of community was a deeply educative process...a reciprocal process...akin to the experience of a theatre audience...The whole process involved a performance by the teacher, a collective, but enjoyed and shared, response from the audience, together with a fair amount of audience participation.

Fleming and Stevens enthusiastically claim that:

This is reading in a celebratory sense, and requires that 'we awaken our faith' in the possibilities of performance and inspiration as central to English teaching. And like any performance, it needs preparation and rehearsal, not least on the part of the teacher. The rewards, however, can be immense, and more or less distinctive to the English classroom.

It seems almost curmudgeonly to suggest that this very self-indulgent approach to shared reading has little, ultimately, to contribute to pupils' improved reading attainment and should be used only sparingly. I do, however, agree with these writers when they recommend that, 'at the very least, reading aloud needs some time for rehearsal', and I think they are referring to pupils in this instance.

Book boxes

Aware that some of their former reading procedures have not led to improved reading engagement and attainment, a large number English departments have explored other ways of bringing their pupils and reading texts into close relationships during the past decade. They have adopted 'book boxes', or similar collections, where a number of individual copies, or small sets, of texts are made available to pupils. These collections might share a thematic relationship, some link might have been made between the different authors or they could contain material regarded as offering good contrasts in attitude, approach or expression. Whatever the connections between the texts in these collections, the teachers have intended that their pupils have far greater choice than might be afforded with the 'class reader'. This sort of provision is more demanding of teacher time, and individual attention has to be given to each pupil, as choices are discussed and negotiated.

There are more chances that personal choices and interests are likely to be met through this method. Collections can be established to meet pupils' suggestions and preferences, with a degree of extra challenge added by the teachers. The follow-up and related work can be more carefully tailored to suit pupil ability. Pupils can form small groups, sharing similar tastes and interests, to read a text together, or they can read alone from choice. Reading aloud with a smaller group is more comfortable for some pupils, who are less willing to participate in a whole-class context. Yet such an arrangement does not of itself mean that there is a greater likelihood of the teaching of reading. To be sure of that taking place, the teachers in the department still have to be working within a structure clearly laid out to bring about improvement, across a number of reading encounters, and have in place the means of checking those improvements.

Book boxes make large, extra demands on teachers' time and organisational powers. They have to monitor more carefully the 'choices' of their pupils. They need to know more about a wider range of texts, to make connections and recommendations designed to help the progression of their pupils. It is not as easy to listen to pupils reading aloud, and the meanings they make of their textual encounters are much more difficult to track. Having established a series of boxes to meet the needs and choices of one year group will not in itself be a guarantee that the following year group will also be similarly served.

Group/guided reading

A few English departments organise reading sessions with small groups of readers collaboratively sharing a text, often allocated to each group at an 'appropriate level of difficulty', although some are allowed choices from a given stock. Most groups comprise pupils of similar reading attainment but, exceptionally, the group could be mixed ability. The teacher might then visit each group on a regular basis, hearing individuals read aloud and discussing with them the development of the plot or other related features.

In secondary schools which have become quickly attuned to the methodologies of the Literacy Strategy, teachers have introduced the 'guided reading' model. Small groups share a text, as described in the preceding paragraph, but the teacher takes a more active role in relation to each group. No longer do they visit to hear readers and to make supportive commentary, but they use their time with each group much more interactively, teaching reading strategies. This way of working demands that the teachers know the texts very well, and are properly prepared for each of their encounters with the pupils. They spend the ten or fifteen minutes with each group, pointing out specific aspects of the text which the readers would be unlikely to find for themselves, as a way of alerting the pupils to these ways of making meaning in the future. Boys experiencing difficulties with reading are often more supported in this sort of reading situation, and make greater progress when their teachers can work more closely alongside them.

Guided reading is not the same as group reading. The time the teacher spends with the group should be an intensive teaching experience. The pupils should leave the encounter with more strategies for making meaning from the text, and be able to apply those strategies to other texts, than they would have developed by themselves. The teacher really has to know the reading attainment of members of the group quite closely to make this method work really well.

Library lessons

Virtually every English department will allocate some time in each week, fortnight or month for the pupils in Key Stage 3 (although not as often in Key Stage 4) to visit the library. These are variously called 'library periods' or 'reading periods', and the name is worth exploring, as it gives clues to the intended activity. The rules governing these periods differ from school to school, but there are sufficient shared practices to allow the description of a fairly common programme. Pupils arrive at the library, make an ordered 'scramble' for seats and settle down with the books they have selected from the library or have brought from home. Those without books, or who have finished the previous one, are allowed a bit of time to select some new reading material. Where a school is lucky enough to be able to employ a librarian, that person will supervise the issuing of texts, and often make recommendations of titles to pupils. In a few schools, pupils then return to their classroom (possibly because the library is already busy with sixth form students studying individually), to read silently. More often the whole class is expected to read silently in the library for however much time remains of the lesson. In some schools quite a number of the classes understand the procedures and comply with the requirements of their teachers, but this practice is by no means commonplace.

Those pupils who are already committed readers are unlikely to offer any problems; they lose themselves in their texts very quickly. There are, however, in different schools, proportions of classes not so committed, pupils who think the library reading lesson a less than absorbing experience. Younger pupils mostly do as they are told, but as they grow older it is not unusual to observe a hard core of more difficult pupils beginning to use these lessons for other, less relevant purposes. Teachers will know of pupils who never bring a book with them, and who 'choose' a different title each week, failing to make any progress beyond the first page – or even the first few words. A few pupils find sustaining concentrated reading for any length of time difficult, and soon become bored. They then use their texts as 'shields' to hide their faces, and particularly their mouths, as they clandestinely communicate with like-minded others. Many English departments have established rules about allowing only fiction texts to be read in the library lesson, which does not suit all readers. This particular rule is understandable, but it is usually not the result of a fully considered and shared reading policy. Many boys, and some girls, are particularly disadvantaged by this directive; they are not naturally interested in fictional texts yet, are unable to involve themselves in reading alternatives, and do not know why they are excluded from them. The distractions often caused by this dissident group regularly make the silent reading experiences of the others difficult to maintain. It could be claimed that the committed readers would have found their own opportunities to read anyway, while nothing has been achieved towards improving the reading of the more reluctant.

The issue of silent reading is explored in more detail in a later section, but it has to be mentioned in this context. Expressed bluntly, silent reading is probably the least accountable activity that an English teacher can conduct. There is simply no way of being able to ascertain the value of what takes place, because the experience is so personal and locked into the heads of each of the participants. If, as happens in some departments, one lesson out of four each week is allocated to silent reading, then one quarter of the available English time has been invested in this enterprise. Such a massive commitment has to be shown to making a significant difference, or it is not worth continuing. Time is so limited in the secondary school and English departments cannot complain about not being given enough if they cannot demonstrate how effectively they are using what they have.

At one extreme there might well be pupils, mostly girls, absorbed in reading, absolutely quiet and involved for the whole reading period. Yet they might not be making any 'progress' at all during that time, assuming that the department has already agreed what 'progress' might mean in the first place. Very able readers can be helped to become even better, but the silent engagement is unable to assure the teacher that such a development is in train. At the other end of the scale are pupils making virtually no engagement at all with the texts in front of them. Their eyes pass over the page, and even try to pick out individual words to search for some connection and fundamental meaning, but they cannot relate the parts to the whole. Left to themselves for 40 minutes or so, all they manage to achieve is the confirmation of their own failure. It is, therefore, not surprising that they seek other, more interesting occupations for silent reading occasions. Ironically, every English department is committed to assisting pupils to read 'for pleasure', yet huge numbers of teachers insist that their pupils take part in this silent reading enterprise whether they like it or not! There is another way of perceiving the same situation. Pupils can only practise reading if they are given the space and time to do so. Teachers could make it their business to monitor the suitability, challenge and likely engagement of the text for individual readers. They might also make positive, carefully gauged interventions in ways designed to encourage greater involvement with the text, and which bring about better understanding. Unfortunately, I have observed more scenes depicting the former situation and, however much departments might aspire to the second setting, they rarely occur.

The library and its place in reading practices

The picture of library lessons described in preceding paragraphs is not true of all schools, but it is common enough to warrant proper attention and raises questions about the place of the library and its facilities in the discussion of teaching reading. Where the library and its functions have been properly integrated into reading policies, they usually have an enormously positive impact. Libraries have the potential to offer a wide range of books to supplement English lessons; they can also be regarded as facilities able to support a number of reading functions. Interactive engagements with texts are given higher priorities in those planned circumstances: pupils might well be provided with a space to discuss their reading and share opinions; the adults present (or, sometimes, older pupil reading mentors) might be helping pupils find their way about the library and individual texts; one or two pupils could possibly be listening to an audio tape of a new or favourite book on headphones; others might be exploring some research on a computer, or even watching a video representation; the librarian conducting a reading interview.

This is a suitable point to mention the role of the school librarian in the school's development of reading purposes. Most librarians are genuinely valued by their schools, and are regarded as wholly intrinsic to the reading development of the pupils; yet some are hidden away in an area called the 'library', and are not invited or expected to contribute to learning and curriculum development. (When shown around an unfamiliar school by a head teacher, I wait to see how much priority is given to the library, and wonder if I will be introduced to the librarian.) An increasingly common indicator of the librarian's function and purpose, these days, is in the title adopted by the school. Some are now called 'Learning Centre Manager', 'Senior Resources Manager', 'Information and Research Manager', and other similar designations, pointing to changes in responsibility and job description.

Librarians, or whatever new designation, can make a significant impact on the reading culture and practices in a school, where they are expected to work alongside teaching colleagues, guiding and contributing to the ways policy is devised and enacted. At the very least, a librarian should be actively collaborating with English department staff at many levels, sharing a portion of meeting time and supporting the teaching of reading in a number of ways. The most effective and influential use I ever saw of a librarian involved that person teaching not only research and library-use lessons, but also preparing different collections of texts to illustrate teaching of reading sessions, supervising the files of pupils' reading recommendations to ensure they were read and seen by others and conducting pupil reading interviews. (These duties were in addition to the other mainstream jobs any librarian might be expected to carry out!) Their skills and expertise should be used to maximum effect wherever possible.

Wider/independent reading

Daly (1999), writing in *The Secondary English Magazine*, states:

The proposed new National Curriculum for September 2000 gives primacy to independent reading: '*During key stages 3 and 4 the emphasis is on encouraging pupils to read a wide range of texts independently, for pleasure and for study.'*

This statement gives rise to questions such as:

- Where is independent reading given real time and status within many English departments today?
- How far can independent reading embrace a range of reading which is hard to achieve by teaching a series of whole-class texts?
- How far can independent reading develop pupils' reading pleasures and capabilities if it exists mostly in marginalised time? Too frequently in lessons it serves as a ten-minute opening, partly to get pupils to be quiet, and is expendable when 'real' work begins.

Independent reading, regarded for so long as a cornerstone of English work, is really so difficult to maintain and incorporate in the overall programme of the department. Every English teacher has the best of intentions about it, but few are able to sustain their initial commitment, and those intentions are regularly honoured in the breach. Yet, no department is capable of studying sufficient numbers of books within the allotted English time.

Everybody concerned with English wants young people to continue to read, to read more challenging texts, to get better at reading and to enjoy reading – all at the same time! It is, however, impossible to ensure that all these important developments are taking place. In some respects, to pursue all those aims all the time is to miss the point about what often takes place in personal reading practices. What place, for instance, would be given to rereading in the above policy? Pleasure is regularly indicated by re-reading (unless the point of the book was missed in the first place!), but can it be regarded as further challenge? Some pupils (especially girls) dutifully read books that are challenging, but they actually give little, ultimate pleasure.

What qualifies for independent reading? Are only books of a certain sort eligible. What might be regarded as 'schooly books'? Does 'independence' really mean total independence of choice, or is there always a degree of intervention implied in the activity? Can the reading be of non-fiction texts – biography, travel or technical texts?

Reading comprehension

In many English departments teachers still feel it is necessary to provide separate 'comprehension' lessons as a way of developing reading skills, although this practice has been diminishing since the 1970s. A glance at most of the English textbooks of those days will show that the 'comprehension' model was predominant, with regular doses of decontextualised passages followed by sets of closed questions being put before the majority of English classes; what Trevor Cairney calls the 'skiller and driller' approach! An advertisement by a publisher in the *TES* in 1999 shows that the practice is not dead. A book with 'basic comprehension skills' in the title is capable of providing: 'a step-by-step route for improving lower-ability students' comprehension skills...helps students tackle fiction, non-fiction, drama and poetry extracts'. The assumptions about reading and the teaching and learning of reading are really worth exploring in such a claim.

Durkin (1979) points out that activities of this kind usually show us nothing more than how well pupils can transfer information from one form to another. Too often this sort of exercise involves little more than moving blocks of text from one line to another, without any sort of intellectual engagement. Most alarming, on occasions when I have observed pupils taking part in compre-hension exercises in classrooms, was the lack of care or involvement by most pupils, who could not even be bothered to copy correctly when transferring words on to their pages from the passage. For the majority of pupils it became a routine time filler in the English classroom, but not much was learned about reading as a consequence. Like all closed questions, the best responders are those pupils who tune into the wavelength of the questioner (in this case the writer of the exercise). As a fairly able reader in my grammar school, I soon worked out that I did not have to read through any passage in order to answer the questions. I merely found the 'cue' words (always in chronological order), and wrote down what followed – always in a proper sentence, of course. I claim that I passed O level English by *not* reading the paper, and I am certain that I was not alone!

While this overt exercise is now practised much less frequently in English lessons, at least in a separate form, this way of supporting the reading of shared texts is still common. Many English departments use this device to 'test' their pupils' reading and some year groups still face 'examinations' at the end of each year, based on these methods. English teachers will, quite reasonably, point to the National Curriculum Key Stage Assessment Tests, and suggest that to omit this model of comprehension from their programme of studies would be to disadvantage pupils in the test situation. I agree with their argument, but wish to offer other evidence about the limited value of such ways of interpreting text as a means of suggesting that it should be used very sparingly; indeed, only as formal practise for the tests themselves. Harrison (1995) comments on the work of Dole and her team in 1991:

> The paper, which was written by some of the most distinguished reading researchers in the US, is fairly dismissive of what have been called 'assembly-line' models of reading comprehension, which date back to the 1950s, and which view reading as a set of sub-skills. Such models would seek to describe readers' abilities in terms of comprehension sub-skills, such as finding out the

main points in a passage, predicting outcomes, drawing conclusions, and so on, which, it was thought, could be tested, developed and mastered independently.

Harrison also points out a weakness articulated by many English teachers: that in this sort of 'testing' what is apparently a test of reading is actually a test of writing. I am not suggesting that teachers should not concern themselves with ascertaining what their pupils are discovering in texts, or that they should not be exploring lines of enquiry together. This is exactly the area of reading activity teachers should be promoting. There is, however, too much writing to little purpose in English classrooms, and one portion which could be judiciously cut is the written comprehension exercise. (Teachers might look at the comprehension writing in pupils' books to see how little meaning it contains after the exercise is finished, and to ask, 'Why is it necessary to keep this?', or even, 'Was it worth writing down in the first place?')

It is often easy to mix up 'response' to literature with an undemanding level of comprehension. I observed an able group of Year 8 pupils reading Roald Dahl's *Boy*. Having been asked to read a vivid passage about one of Dahl's teachers, a former army officer, whom he clearly hated, they were then asked to write three paragraphs: 'what was Captain ....'s appearance?', 'what was Captain ...'s behaviour?', 'would you have liked Captain ...?' Considerations of the language Dahl employed to make plain his contempt for this character were wholly neglected in this sort of exercise, and all the pupils wrote a banal piece, exactly mirroring the limited interpretation determined by the teacher. Such approaches suggest to pupils that readers need only activate very restricted lines of enquiry in regard to textual material, and they soon lose any desire to demonstrate their insights about the excitement a text might possibly engender.

Poetry

The National Curriculum 'Reading' Orders, outlining the statutory requirements for pupils in secondary schools, are written to cover Key Stages 3 *and* 4, with no recommendation about which materials might be suitable for a particular age group. The poetry syllabus can, therefore, be introduced to pupils at any time between the ages of 11 and 16, and still meet the legal specifications. A considerable number of English departments try to maintain a balance in their reading curriculum, and revisit different forms of poetry at various stages during their pupils' secondary life.

Yet not every English department teaches poetry in Key Stage 3, and some departments teach it only cursorily. One of my own children read *The Highwayman* by Alfred Noyes in Year 9, performed a comprehension exercise on it and took part in a short discussion related to it. Until he encountered the dramatic verse (unfortunately, not a quality actually highlighted in the language!) of *Romeo and Juliet* a few months later, for testing purposes, that was the totality of his poetic experience between the ages of 11 and 14.

Poetry is thought to be too difficult for many young people and some English teachers, realising that boys do not readily absorb themselves in poetry, or any piece of writing which resembles verse, simply avoid it. Most pupils entering secondary school until very recently have only the scantiest knowledge of poetry, as their encounters in primary schools have been so limited, or they have learned some extraordinary 'rules' which do not readily translate into further study. (The National Literacy Strategy should bring about an improvement in this state of affairs.) A few secondary teachers have settled for a compromise: knowing that introducing certain forms of poetry will be a struggle, they have selected 'lighter' verse from anthologies, or they devise units of haiku, acrostics or caligrams because they provide, apparently, greater structure. There might even be study of ballads, because they can be related to current events ('The ballad of Princess Diana' is a recent favourite of pupil balladeers) and are built on recognisable organisational patterns.

Some teachers, of course, are enthusiasts. Far from being deterred by the linguistic density of poetry, they actually make its complexities an important feature for study. For such an approach to be successful demands great determination and careful planning by the teacher, as well as a belief that the pupils have the capacity to make something worthwhile of the experience. Some years ago I worked with a group of newly qualified teachers in Oxfordshire who were interested in pursuing some difficult poetic ideas with pupils. One produced a unit of very demanding work about comparing sonnets through the ages, enjoyed by a mixed ability group of Year 8 pupils, able to speak confidently about their studies at its conclusion. Teachers who engage their pupils fully in this area of study are likely to begin from a position that regards no text as being beyond the grasp of their pupils. The real problem, as they understand it, is determining the correct level of support necessary to make that text offer sufficient meaning to that particular reader.

This most personal way of responding to reading is so thoroughly dependent on pupils' commitment to the text and its language that it particularly highlights the difficulties all reading presents. Unfortunately, the extent of study often does not develop beyond using poetry as a starting point for comprehension exercises (at its worst, presented through pursuits such as 'spotting the metaphors'), or for a whole variety of 'reconstruction' activities (e.g. poems cut up into single lines or stanzas, and pupils asked to place them in order – not in itself a worthless exercise, but not always developed much beyond the reconstruction), or for attempted 'immersion', before expecting pupils to write their own examples. All of these peripheral enterprises are genuinely meant procedures for assisting pupils to find their way into the text; unfortunately, they usually have the opposite effect. They take up too much time, leaving none for exploring the sort of involvement intended. They skirt around the outside or surface of the text, without challenging the reader to enter. Ultimately they fail to invite the pupil to speculate about what the poet set out to communicate; why the writer employed the vocabulary, structure and effects that make the poem what it is and the resonances likely to be made by the reader as the poem is urged to unravel its meanings.

Because of these less than wholehearted approaches, poetry remains a strictly minority interest for most young people. The total poetic knowledge of even prospective A level English literature students might be little more than the study of five or six poems by, for instance, Seamus Heaney or Wilfred Owen, packaged in a selection of different poems from a GCSE anthology.

Little surprise that Hall and Coles (1999), in their study of the reading habits of 12-14 year old pupils, can confidently report:

> The poetry reading figures relating to age show an enthusiasm for reading poetry in 10-year-olds which has declined sharply by 12 and has all but disappeared by 14.

Specific lessons: study of non-fiction

Non-fiction material has been a feature of English lessons for many years. The English National Curriculum Orders (DfE 1995) requires study of: '...a wide range of non-fiction texts e.g. *autobiographies, biographies, journals, diaries, letters, travel writing, leaflets...*', with pupils 'given opportunities to read texts that show quality in language use...', and 'pupils should be introduced to a wide range of media, e.g. *magazines, Newspapers, radio, television, film.*' As long as it is 'of high quality'!

Newspapers, magazines, leaflets, programmes, brochures, posters, flyers, junk mail and all sorts of everyday textual material have been used as study material and stimulus for own writing for many years in English classrooms. These published works might be employed to illustrate how arguments and points of view are constructed by journalists and other writers, or they could be used as examples of persuasive and evocative language. Pupils are usually assisted through some study of one of these pieces and then expected to construct a similar text for themselves. Occasionally they might compare one piece with another, or make a set of statements about a common topic through constructing a range of texts, as a way of comparing. Too often, however, the actual making and completion of a 'copy' text is more important than accurately recapturing the linguistic characteristics of the original.

We know from studies, such as Hall and Coles (1999), that pupils in secondary schools read huge numbers of newspapers and periodicals. Indeed, the study discovered that young people read more magazines than books. Certainly, the shelves of any newsagent bear testimony to the enormous explosion of publishing, specifically for younger readers, which has characterised the last few years. Hall and Coles have found that whereas girls would once regularly read the magazines published for their mothers, they now read copies of titles exclusively aimed at targeted age groups. Boys, too, enjoy a vast range of specialist sport, hobbies, wargaming, computer and lifestyle magazines. As Reynolds (1995), Inspector for English in Tower Hamlets, has commented:

> Beyond fiction boys read considerably more factually based texts, often for information about particular enthusiasms such as computer games or sport and pastimes (not only football, but also fishing, for example). Again, English stock cupboards are hardly groaning under the weight of non-fiction texts which meet the requirements of the National Curriculum order, let alone are current and new and related to such interests of boys.

As a few secondary schools have begun to acknowledge the vital role they have to play in developing and improving their pupils' overall literacy attainment, so they have looked again at the middle management responsibilities of their staff. Recent job advertisements for Head of English posts have increasingly made reference to the expectation of the successful post holder taking a leading position in the school for the introduction and development of whole-school literacy practices.

In these circumstances, Heads of English have initiated or taken part in a growing number of cross-departmental discussions, where examination of the range of text types routinely employed in all subjects of the school curriculum has become the shared area of interest. Realising that pupils need to have greater knowledge of these text types through longer acquaintance than can be afforded in the subject lessons themselves, there has been further study of a range of these texts in English lessons. This practice is not yet common, but there is likely to be a growing pressure on the English department to offer a 'background language' course, designed to give greater coherence to the diverse language demands of the whole curriculum. Many teachers of English actually know little about the nature of a broader literacy, and their own training needs are sometimes the same as those of colleagues from other departments.

Anticipating this development, some secondary schools have recently introduced a 'literacy hour' based on the model in primary schools, or something like it, as an extra language focus for pupils in Year 7. This hour has not always been taken from allocated English curriculum space, but found from other subject time. Yet most of these courses have been wholly or partially staffed by English teachers, even though the material being studied might not be regarded as 'English'. Pupils have been expected to read more closely and ask analytical questions of their wider reading across the whole curriculum in the best of these courses, but their consistent quality has yet to be properly established in quite a lot of schools.

Visual media

Television and film have also been included in the textual study programme of English classrooms for a long time, some stalwart film addicts showing film on unreliable, clanking large reels through projectors in classrooms in the 1960s. Since the coming of video, film and television have both become commonplace in English lessons, but these visual texts are not regularly studied or 'read' in great detail. They are more likely to be shown to 'animate' the written text, which is mostly regarded as being the 'superior' version. So, since the introduction of the Key Stage 3 test, it has become almost compulsory to see a video version of Franco Zeffirelli's film version of *Romeo and Juliet* playing in Year 9 lessons. That filmic interpretation has more recently been replaced by Baz Lurhmann's production, but neither version has been looked at closely in many classrooms, to discover what each might tell us about how we reproduce 'classical' texts in the images of our own times.

It is also usual for English teachers to show the filmed versions of literary texts for classes they believe might encounter difficulties in understanding context and setting of the original, or who might find the language particularly dense and unfamiliar. *To Kill a Mocking Bird* is very popular with Year 9 and 10 pupils, and part of its lasting charm has to do with the character of Scout, with whom young readers feel an immediate sympathy. Yet the racist pre-war southern United States' setting is unknown to most pupils, and the 1962 film directed by Robert Mulligan offers a sense of the times not available in any other way. Similarly, Peter Brook's vivid adaptation of *Lord of the Flies* helps pupils to understand something of the claustrophobic, psychological metaphors employed by Golding. David Lean's fine evocation of Dickens's *Great Expectations* offers a clear plot outline for less confident readers even today, fifty years after it was made. The films are so helpful and absorbing that pupils even make allowances for the fact that all three examples were shot in black and white!

Unfortunately, when these visual examples are shown in classrooms, they are usually passed through as quickly as possible without planned time made available to 'read' them in a similar way as the original literary text. To invest some time into considering why film makers have chosen to employ particular images, settings, *mise en scène*, edits, lighting and other visual devices is as important to the conveying of full meaning as studying the language of the book. To see something of the intentions of the director of the film, is to gain further insights into the written text. In an increasingly visual textual age, schools have to validate and promote reading learning in visual media. Pupils need to progress in their understanding of the construction, purposes, genres and meaning-making of these texts. Outside school young people 'consume' huge quantities of visual texts, often watching them but not so frequently engaging with them. If one of the functions of the school is to increase the knowledge pupils have of issues impacting on their lives, which they would be unlikely to discover unaided, then the visual texts they encounter qualify just as surely as their printed counterparts.

Drama-based activities

The National Curriculum expects English departments to incorporate drama activities into their programmes of work, and some teachers are able to make these a natural part in the further making of textual meaning. Activities include 'hot seating', 'thought tracking', 'conscience alley' or 'mantle of the expert', all in their ways inviting the pupil to adopt an 'in role' stance in relation to the text being read. Through these devices pupils are drawn more closely into the events of the book by being invited to see events and dilemmas from the point of view of the featured characters.

It is more helpful to the English teacher if these approaches are already familiar to the pupils, either through previous lessons or because they are customarily employed in drama lessons. They demand a high level of pupil commitment and belief to work effectively, and can quickly be subverted by a less than secure group. Properly understood and used by teacher and pupils, however, they can be powerful ways of making closer engagements with texts.

The most usual way of involving drama in the English classroom, is through the reading aloud of a drama text. Pupils often enjoy this activity, and it can be a very effective way of encouraging the more reluctant pupils to read, as they might only need to attempt a few words at a time. One of the major problems encountered by English teachers is the paucity of texts suitable for Key Stage 3 pupils. It is usual for GCSE courses to include adult drama texts in their syllabuses, but these can be too demanding for some junior, inexperienced readers. Recently, published dramatisations of popular novels written for pupils in this age group have become available, serving two good purposes: allowing pupils better access to dramatic form and supporting reading of prose texts. Conducted well, with a bit of time for rehearsal and preparation, play texts can be a valuable way of helping a large number of pupils become more successful in searching for meaning in collaboration.

It is impossible at this stage not to mention Shakespeare. Since the introduction of Key Stage 3 assessment tests all Year 9 pupils have had to study at least a few scenes from a Shakespeare play in order to answer a few comprehension questions in examination conditions. That English teachers have managed to maintain a mostly positive pupil reaction to Shakespeare under these circumstances has been remarkable. Difficult text has been brought alive and made relevant in many ingenious ways; but the utterly limited possibilities of pupil response in examinations for these pupils have continued to confirm a narrow view of reading in the English classroom.

Reading logs/reading records/reading reviews

Records ought to be kept of what pupils read, but teachers would find it unreasonably difficult to keep up with this form of record-keeping, so the best solution is to ask the pupils to maintain their own logs. Yet many pupils see this particular task as a tedious and unnecessary chore. They do not really know what the teacher wants them to record, they are given little modelling of the sorts of entries they should be making and they do not like having to make a written statement every time they finish a book. Reading records / logs are often the embodiment of teachers' good intentions in the early part of the autumn term, but the entries gradually decline as Christmas approaches, and they disappear altogether in the new year. Teachers have explored all sorts of alternative ways to make these records have greater applicability, but they are frequently not maintained.

It can be difficult to decide how much detail ought to be included to make these records valid and developmental. Too much and pupils dislike them; too little and they become merely tokenistic. Most pupils, asked to write about the fictional books they have read, relate the main outlines of the plot, and add a little afterthought, such as, 'I recommend this book to other readers.' In fairness, the vast majority of pupils have never been taught how to construct a review, nor to consider what function it is meant to be performing. A few reading records require pupils to make a next step by classifying their books into genres, but they are not asked to make further judgements or comparisons based on those classifications. A number of pupils are urged to apply numerical grades to books read, on perhaps a 1–10, or 1–5 scale. It is not unusual to find reading records that degenerate into merely the book title, accompanied by a number. The very worst records record no more than the book's title, followed by a word, such as, 'brilliant', 'exciting' or 'boring' and – in extreme cases – a smiley face indicating different degrees of pleasure related to the engagement!

Like all writing, these records need an audience to give them real validity. Teachers do occasionally read through them, but for the most part once they are written they become dead material. Recognising that book reviews should be more interactive, a number of teachers and librarians have devoted a small portion of the library to displaying pupils' judgements of books. These different ways of recording range from dedicated computer programs accessible to all readers, wall displays of the latest reviews, to the production of booklets, like photograph albums, left about the library for pupils to consult. While these appraisals can serve the purpose of encouraging others to attempt titles they might not have otherwise discovered, they do not also serve their other purpose of giving the teachers a proper insight into the reading abilities or growth of their pupils. The best reviews are mostly written by those pupils with already developed accomplished writing skills, yet they do not necessarily indicate reading growth.

SQUIRT (Silent Quiet Uninterrupted Intensive Reading Time) / USSR (Uninterrupted Silent Solo Reading) / ERIC (Everyone Reading In Class) / DEAR (Drop Everything And Read) and similar acronyms!

Meek (1996) has argued that:

> ... every school has a view of literacy, not always explicit. The nature of the provisions: lessons, books, visiting experts, materials, announces the policy, the theoretical substructure, the concern of the institution for reading and writing. In facing outwards to the community, the school announces its view of literacy, at least partly, by the allocation of place, time, people and resources to bring it about.

Working on these principles, a number of schools have introduced strategies to make their statements about literacy absolutely explicit. One of these innovations has been the introduction of a shared reading session, involving a whole year group, and in a few instances even the whole school, being expected to read silently for an allocated period of time on a regular basis. Staff, non-teaching assistants and administrators have also been required to read, as a way of 'modelling' adult reading behaviours. (But how is an adult able to 'model' good silent reading behaviour to any real effect? The pupils, at best, can only witness an adult sitting quietly, reading, seemingly involved in the text. The pupils are unlikely to see any personal response taking place, nor will they detect any clues worth applying to their own reading. This phenomenon of an adult sitting reading might be an unusual sight for some pupils from backgrounds where adults do not naturally involve themselves in texts – but its impact must be limited and hardly sustainable for a lengthy period of time.)

Clipson-Boyles (1995) points out:

> An eleven-year-old pupil was asked recently what he thought about USSR (Uninterrupted Sustained Silent Reading) by a teacher who was beginning to have doubts about the efficacy of that particular school policy. His honest and prompt answer was brief and to the point: 'No-one reads!'

Secondary schools have to realise that many pupils have been expected to work in this way for the past six years, and they have never enjoyed it or ever had the real point of the exercise pointed out to them. To be asked, as if it is a new idea, to renew their engagements with texts in this already discredited manner is unlikely to be met with a positive response. Teachers might have to 'retrain' their readers to take on this commitment if they want it to work well.

Such clear pronouncements of a school's commitment to reading have been successful where they have been sustained, but they do call for a huge investment of teacher belief and good will in the initiative. More often, smaller scale whole-year, or whole-school, shared reading programmes occur during identified tutor times where they are easier to manage. They still, nevertheless, require the tutor to have sufficient conviction in the enterprise, to prevent using the time for other, usually administrative, activities, when their distractions could well spoil the point of the exercise. There also has to be an agreement about what is and what is not allowed in the circumstances of this reading. For instance:

- Are pupils allowed to read anything, or are they restricted to fiction texts?
- Can the pupils bring their own texts (including comics and magazines), or will the materials always be supplied by the school?
- What sort of provision is made for those pupils who 'forget' to bring a text with them? Do they have to go through a 'token' reading exercise, with a text they are unlikely to encounter again?
- What sort of provision is made for pupils who have difficulties with reading? Do they have to plod on with their reading, unsupported, or should they be 'reading' in a more supervised way?
- What is the reading for? Is it expected to be for pleasure, or are pupils able to use the reading time to undertake other activities (such as seeking information to record in various ways)?

These sorts of questions must already have been asked and answered before a school can confidently embark on such a programme with a real expectation of improving the reading pleasures and attainment of large numbers of pupils.

When considering the sorts of reading taking place in library lessons (see earlier section) I raised the issues of 'accountability', and suggested that 'silent reading' is not a suitable way of deploying much English curriculum time. It is quite usual for English teachers to begin lessons with a few minutes of individual, silent reading, before starting on some class enterprise. It can provide an excellent opportunity for teachers to monitor quickly the reading choices of their pupils. Yet some pupils actually object to these short bursts of reading, disliking the inevitable interruption they will experience only moments after settling themselves into the text. I have heard some express their unhappiness about being made to 'read to order'. On the other hand, requiring pupils to travel about the school with a reading book in their bags does make explicit a clear expectation that they should have selected a text to be available at all times. That sort of demand eventually becomes a natural way of life for members of the school, often bringing about a positive reading ethos

Book weeks/bookshops/bookclubs

Some schools go out of their way to bring pupils and books together, recognising that pupils will not find what they might like unless they have plenty of opportunities to sample. Publishers and bookselling organisations are aware of this developing trend in many places, providing packages of books and accompanying artefacts, such as audio tapes, video tapes and other marketing accessories associated with popular texts, or those in the news. This can certainly be a successful way of encouraging reading, and for many young people it provides their first opportunity to purchase their own copies of books. An article in the TES in July 1998 described a Liverpool comprehensive school winning money from a charity, and inviting some of their boys to visit the local Waterstone's to choose books; for many boys their first ever trip inside a bookshop.

The pupils' purchases during these events can be very illuminating. They buy large quantities of 'Horrible Histories', 'Goosebumps' and other series books, not always available on the shelves of the school library. Many boys will choose small non-fiction texts, filled with short paragraphs of specialist information, or books of lists. Sometimes a publishing phenomenon that satisfies the tastes of both pupils and teachers will become fashionable; Philip Pullman's trilogy, *His Dark Materials*, particularly the first work, *Northern Lights,* is a good example, and the Harry Potter series is a more recent instance.

In a few schools it can be a responsibility of a junior member of the English department to run a regular bookshop. The school invests in a number of texts, sometimes curriculum-related, which it sells at a regular time. There might be a few books of more general interest, and orders for particular requirements can be processed, perhaps from samples displayed in a catalogue or single copies available for perusal. Pupils are occasionally able to pay in small amounts of pocket money over a period of weeks for their purchases. This arrangement can be a method of supplementing the department's capitation grant, because booksellers will reward selling outlets with discounts. Where this facility works successfully everybody can benefit: young people will have been encouraged to develop book browsing habits, it can offer further opportunities for pupils and adults to interact together with texts, and the department can afford more resources.

The Liverpool school mentioned in a previous paragraph was also developing an increasingly popular extra-curricular activity: an out of hours reading club. Running this sort of amenity takes more effort by staff than might at first be anticipated but, properly supervised, can result in some real enthusiasm. In the best of these clubs pupils are able to choose ways of reading that suit them: in pairs, in small groups, individually, either in silence or out loud. Sometimes less confident readers are invited to attend and carefully guided towards a more accomplished reader to share a text. There could possibly be a 'recommendations' session, the librarian or a teacher might lead a 'what's new' session and groups of pupils interested in the same hobbies or interests have a chance to explore the available materials they might share. I have seen, in an excellently run reading club, pupils arranging themed book displays, cataloguing book reviews and poring over a published booklet of new texts to select new acquisitions. Some were also reading!

Reading buddies/partners/mentors

A growing trend has been the assigning of new pupils to older pupils, or those of their own peer group, for shared reading sessions. Some schools began this practice as a way of encouraging less confident readers to read with purpose and as a way of helping them make progress. Because of its success, there are now instances where the pairing of pupils has been extended across whole year groups, offering benefit to more than just the least accomplished. A few English departments, as a way of teaching broader language studies to their older pupils at GCSE or A level, have also set up units of work involving the pupils working alongside younger members of the school to evaluate their reading skills, and supply necessary assistance. I have also seen sixth form students performing 'community service' activities in their schools by accompanying junior classes to their library or silent reading sessions, and working alongside the pupils, listening to them read and helping them make book choices. Interestingly, these ideas have often made a real impact in boys' schools, and brought about some improved changes in relations between age groups as a result. Hearing some very large Year 11 lads talking about 'my reader' in Year 7 in a supportive and protective manner can be most heartening!

This sort of activity needs considerable planning and organisation to be truly successful, but there are some excellent schemes in operation. Schools have come up with many different ways of making this valuable collaborative enterprise come alive. They might allocate a paired reading time, for 15–20 minutes one day each week, after morning registration. Groups of pupils meet older mentors at agreed points around the school, with their texts. They read these aloud to their partners, sometimes stopping to talk about issues or points requiring further attention. The best support is given when teachers have managed to set up this interaction with a little preparatory 'training'; mentors having been given suggestions about prompting and probing their readers' knowledge and interest. Sometimes, a school will arrange for the least able to benefit from this extra attention; a few have determined that all Year 8 and Year 9 pupils should be entitled to this assistance.

The criteria for selecting mentors differ from school to school. In some, the more able readers in Years 10 and 11 are selected or encouraged to be paired with less confident younger pupils. In others, any older pupil is eligible to become a mentor, and in those situations where a whole year group is supporting a younger one, everybody has to take part. This last arrangement can lead to some surprising and encouraging, often unforeseen, benefits. Teachers have told me of underachieving Year 11 pupils, particularly boys, who have taken a far greater interest in the whole process of reading because of their involvement with a younger pupil, causing them to reflect more directly on their own textual experiences. Through their efforts of attempting to help others make meaning, they have themselves developed better reading strategies.

When considering how to make schools more supportive and influential literacy environments, school management teams should spend some time considering these new developments. The investment of a portion of the week to this very active attention to reading could be worthwhile for many, yielding better results than might originally be anticipated.

Shadowing the Carnegie Award and other publishing related exercises

Every year the Youth Libraries Group, one of the Library Association's special interest groups, draws up a shortlist of nominated books for children published during the previous year, thought worthy of the Carnegie Medal. This shortlisting process usually takes place in early May, followed by the announcement of a winner in July. For the past few years it has been possible for a school to register with the Library Association to 'shadow' the scheme. Registered schools are sent a package by the Association, including the titles of shortlisted books immediately after selection. The school is then expected to purchase a few copies of each work, to ensure that groups of readers have an opportunity to read most or all of the books, and to organise a voting procedure to select a 'winner', before the Association's own announcement. The groups of readers taking part might be self-selecting, they could be a class or group of more able readers, or the reading club members.

Increasing numbers of schools have been conducting this 'shadowing' exercise and there is almost as much eagerness about awaiting the shortlist in schools as there is amongst librarians. It is an illuminating activity for young people to participate in. They are, after all, encouraged to read a number of books in a limited time. They have to read with alert critical faculties, because they will be asked to make real judgements about their reading, and they are constantly comparing the different books under consideration. But potentially the most interesting and developmental aspect of the initiative is the sorts of talk and issues into which these pupils can be drawn. Is their own choice in line with those of their peers? What are the differences of opinion in the school itself? Are the votes of the pupils in line with those of the adult judges? Do the tastes of adults (including their teachers) and pupils coincide? Why might these books have been chosen in the first place? What sorts of books never seem to reach shortlists of this kind? Are the shortlists of the Carnegie award similar to the *Guardian*'s Children's Fiction Award or the Whitbread Literary Award Children's Novel lists? To what extent are these awards really publishers' ventures and part of the bookselling trade? How have the award winners changed over the years since the Carnegie Award was instated in the 1930s? Which past award winning titles have remained popular, or even read, since their initial success?

These wider areas of discussion about books and reading are not those which often crop up in English lessons, because English teachers feel under an obligation to ensure their pupils are more actively particpating in actual textual engagements. But time should be found to help pupils reflect on the sorts of choices often being made on their behalf. As suggested in the section on 'The Class Reader', enormous assumptions are often being made about the pupils and their interests, the sorts of texts likely to make an impact on them and the whole business of reading. Enormous numbers of young people, it would seem from the study of their reading habits conducted by Collins *et al.* (1997), think of reading as an activity sanctioned by school and not something they wish to do on their own behalf. If the pupils are not naturally reading of their own volition, and for many the only reading they do actually takes place in school, then even greater importance becomes attached to the choices made for them.

Reading 'challenges'

A few schools make clear their reading expectations very early to pupils in their intake year by providing booklets with suggested reading activities to be undertaken during the year. Some of these activities will be directly related to reading activities in English lessons, but some will be used for homework, and the rest to support pupils' spare time reading. The booklets set out ways in which pupils can more actively explore many different sorts of text: novels recommended by the school, novels chosen by the reader from a range of genres – comics, magazines, newspapers, the internet, poetry, non-fiction – with some room for reflection of what has been read.

The 'challenges' will not perform their jobs very effectively unless they continue to be referred to and monitored by staff during the school year, but they do make clear the reading expectations of an English department. They can be developed to form the centrepiece of work for small groups, offering an agenda for discussion about texts, and allowing pupils to see the reading growth of their classmates. Teachers, too, can quickly reach for the evidence they offer about pupils' reading development, and should be able to track the progress of the responses being made. Some booklets make it possible for pupils to claim rewards after completing a range of tasks, and these are possible to achieve regardless of ability.

Parents as reading partners

Most pupils in primary schools are expected to take home a reading text nearly every evening, to share with an adult or to be read alone. The parents or carers are, at least, aware through this routine that reading is an activity in which they can play a collaborative role with the school. As soon as pupils move to secondary school this relationship of home/school reading usually ceases. I know of a handful of schools who have determined to capitalise on this already existing relationship and extend it for a few more years. The school makes it clear that all pupils are expected to continue reading at home, and parents and carers are given advice about those ways in which they can assist and monitor their children.

It is, of course, not possible to launch such an enterprise without having made careful preparations. Either at the parents' induction meeting, or very early in the child's first term, the English department or school senior manager has to explain to parents what is expected, the intentions of the scheme, their own part in it and the possible achievements. This explanation is more likely to have greater weight in schools where some form of reading policy has already been established and parents can be shown what personal reading means in that context. Most parents are unlikely to know much about reading, and practices will have changed considerably since their own school days, although most will want to support their children's school. Giving the parents a clearer idea of what the school wants to promote is also an important way of supporting pupils' self-evaluation.

Conclusion

Although I have attempted to describe and comment on the most common ways in which teachers bring their pupils into contact with texts in English lessons, there are many I may not have heard about or included. There are bound to be a number of schools who have proudly devised activities or projects designed to improve their pupils' reading that have not received a mention. I hope so.

My purpose for conducting a lightning tour of these reading pursuits is to make the firm point that not all the familiar practices taking place in classrooms have been carefully thought through, and there has been little consideration of their likely effectiveness. As secondary schools begin to respond to the government's requirement that they take a bigger responsibility for improving their pupils' literacy attainment, it is essential that any new reading developments adopted have been properly assessed. I have already heard of schools introducing silent reading sessions, because 'somebody has heard that they increase reading ability', without a full understanding of the implications. Disgruntled pupils and unconvinced staff can quickly sabotage such an unprepared enterprise. The particular experiment is then declared unsuccessful, and abandoned – with it, the school's commitment to enhancing literacy! Just because reading appears to go on does not mean it is making any impact. Reading is too important to be left to chance.

Chapter 3
Making the Case for Teaching Reading

> Reading plays a particularly important role in education. Not only does our education system demand a lot of reading in the process of learning, it also tends to use the capacity to read fluently as an indicator of more general intellectual ability. This tendency to assess intellect through reading is misplaced but prevalent and therefore cannot be ignored. It is part of the function ascribed to literacy, albeit one we need to resist and reform. (Traves 1994)

In the Introduction I attempted to explore the complex relationship currently developing in secondary schools between the subject English and the notion of 'literacy'. Teachers, parents, society in general, and even most pupils, agree that the requirement to be literate in our society is a precondition of further and developing success. (Most young people have no trouble in recognising how vital being 'literate' is; a disturbingly large number, however, have given up what they regard as an unequal struggle by the early stages of secondary education.) One of the central features common to notions of both subject English and literacy is the ability to read. This chapter will be concerned with outlining the secondary school's responsibility for ensuring that reading is not just taking place, but being actively taught in ways it can be sure will have real effect.

Chapter 1 described enormous numbers of reading activities taking place in thousands of schools, not always designed to contribute to the progressive growth of readers. If many of those activities had a clearer focus, a school would be able to articulate specifically the ways by which it is intending to make a positive difference to the reading attainment of its pupils, and produce some evidence to show that, indeed, it has done so.

The commitment to the teaching of reading, and the careful monitoring of the learning resulting from it, will need careful preliminary preparations involving all members of staff. Legislating for reading is not an easy matter, unless some of the complexities of the reading process have already been sufficiently explored and understood. Reading, and thus the teaching of reading, like all other areas of linguistic education are not value-free and, therefore, they are not possible to tackle without shared institutional 'positions' having been determined. Reading practices are only ever constructed through contextual and cultural settings; those contexts have to be established and practised consistently if pupils are not to experience mixed messages (Peim 1993).

> Whatever the situation – of a department, of a school, or within an individual teacher's classroom – ideas about reading, what it is and what it is for, will be a force within the institution, will influence practices and are quite likely to be deeply ingrained...

It is possible that the position a school might come to adopt as a result of subjecting the topic of reading to some careful analysis could directly conflict with current accepted practices, causing staff to feel uncertain about how worthwhile any change would be.

It is not my intention to explore in any detail the growing backdrop of literary and cultural theory currently being increasingly acknowledged and adopted by those concerned with the academic study of English. Put as simply as possible, for the benefit of non-specialist readers, all reading practices are dependent on an ideological position. Reading is only possible to define in political and cultural circumstances, and it is possible to direct or frame reading to fulfil certain institutional aims.

> In schools and in English the ideological aspect of literacy is most often concealed. It could even be said that the business of English in schools is, partly, to conceal the ideological component of literacy. The very idea that there is something called literature, the idea that there are literary texts, the idea that reading is in itself enriching, for example, are all, of course, socially, ideologically produced ideas.... Teaching 'literacy' could well involve some examination of the *idea* of literacy...

Indeed, the history of reading illustrates perfectly how particular power groups have been able to control reading for their own purposes. The early years of the nineteenth century were filled with debate in aristocratic, landed and moneyed circles about the possible social dangers of 'allowing' the proletariat to attend school, with the awful consequences of large numbers of young people learning to read and, possibly, challenging the established social order with their newly acquired knowledge. Before the middle of the ninetenth century, the only reading material taught to the majority of children lucky enough to receive reading tuition was Biblical in origin and it was mostly read to be remembered. Even today, in other parts of the world, many young people are taught to read in practices bearing little relationship with those in British infants schools. Indeed, some Muslim children currently in our schools during the day will attend further sessions in the evenings and at weekends at the mosque, led by a cleric, learning by heart large sections of the Koran.

The resources selected for reading curriculum programmes will always depend on political choices. In the 1990s, most teachers of English feel hampered by the weight of a pre-twentieth-century list of authors, imposed by a Conservative government dedicated to promoting what the Cox Committee called a 'cultural heritage' model of reading. As Wilks (1998) points out:

> Although there have been attempts to justify the reading curriculum by describing it as an 'entitlement curriculum', it is clear that pupils are entitled only to the curriculum chosen for them by politicians and bureaucrats nostalgic for their own schooldays. 'Read what you're given' is the order of the day. At times it feels as if to be an English teacher is to be a collaborator in the imposition of an alien culture which is excluding pupils, sometimes physically.

This imposition was thought necessary to stem a growing tide of internationalism and multiculturalism during the late 1980s, when Britain's national fate began an inexorable shift towards Europe. It was also a time when literary theory began to threaten the previously certain, formerly unquestioned, understandings of what constituted 'literature'. Post-modernist interpretations and perspectives were challenging the privileged status of English literary texts, to the alarm of politicians increasingly concerned about threats to British nationhood. So schools were saddled with a reading curriculum more in keeping with raising, in Victorian social terms, the literary aspirations of young people destined to service the end of the industrial revolution, rather than expecting our educated youth to develop the necessary awareness, flexibility and receptive tolerance to embrace a coming reading revolution.

If schools are to improve their pupils' literacy, they will need to teach reading. But the teaching of reading cannot have real impact, unless the teachers involved have some sense of the difficulties reading presents and are prepared for them. It is an area of educational experience fraught with problems. The following definitions of literacy begin to offer an idea of what I mean:

1. Literacy is the ability to read and use written information and to write appropriately, in a range of contexts. It is used to develop knowledge and understanding, to achieve personal growth and to function effectively in our society. Literacy also includes the recognition of numbers and basic mathematical signs and symbols in texts.

   Literacy involves the integration of speaking, listening, and critical thinking with reading and writing. Effective literacy is intrinsically purposeful, flexible and dynamic and continues to develop through an individual's lifetime.

   (DEET 1992)

2. Literacy involves the integration of listening, speaking, reading and writing and critical thinking. It includes the cultural which enables a speaker, writer or reader to recognise and use language appropriate to different social

situations. Literacy allows people to use language to enhance their capacity to think, to create and question, which helps them to become more aware of the world and empowers them to participate more effectively in society.

(UNESCO 1990)

3. What is clear about literacy is that one learns it within a social context, as an extension of relationships with other people. Hence, the meanings we construct as we read and write are always relative. What we think we know can never be removed from the social context within which we have come to know. All texts are implicated by social relations. We learn to read and write by being apprenticed to a social group.

The meanings we construct as we read and write reflect who we are, what we have experienced, what we know about language and the world, and also our purposes for creating them in the first place. Types of discourse and the way we read or write are the social constructs of specific groups. Individuals are encultured into these practices and meanings. As we make meaning in reading and writing, we do so in relation to other people. (Cairney 1995)

4. Literacy unites the important skills of reading and writing. It also involves speaking and listening...   (DfEE 1998)

Too many teachers in the primary and secondary phases, who have had little time to reflect on the matter in detail, think that 'reading is reading is reading', a practice which takes place regularly and in many ways in school, but which does not require much close scrutiny. In fact, for some teachers of subjects other than English in the secondary school reading as an identified activity worthy of attention simply does not exist. This view cannot be sustained. Reading can only be improved in an atmosphere and ethos capable of addressing some of the many problems it constantly presents.

A simple illustration of the current political and cultural controversy reading is capable of generating can be evidenced in the continuing internecine dispute about just one tiny aspect of the teaching of reading – phonics. Secondary teachers might be astonished to realise how much passion, heat and sheer bitterness is generated by this topic in different political and educational circles, and the introduction of the National Literacy Strategy has provided another opportunity for the revival of old arguments. During the implementation year of the Strategy, 1998 to 1999, an article 'proving' the correctness of one phonics approach or another, appeared in the *TES* almost weekly!

Phonics, the association of sounds with letter symbols, has been the battleground of different political interpretations of the teaching of reading for many decades; it is not a new phenomenon (Harrison and Coles (1992) quote Jagger (1929): 'The teaching of reading to little children has been a scholastic battleground for generations, a battleground that is strewn with lost causes and exploded delusions'.

The proponents of phonics being taught and learned as a necessary prerequisite to the broader teaching of reading often espouse right of centre political views. Many in this 'camp' believe that reading has a systematic basis, and guiding pupils along controlled and clearly defined pathways through its incremental stages will lead to inevitable success. Those who claim that learning to read depends on a wider whole-text understanding, which can be encouraged by an 'immersion' in texts, tend to be regarded as more liberal in their political philosophies. They are often depicted as indulging children, irresponsibly allowing them to take their time in early reading engagements, seeking ways to encourage enjoyment and pleasure at the expense of knuckling down to tackling actual decoding skills. The reality is, as is true of most disputes, that both extreme positions are equally unhelpful. An exclusively phonics-based programme will not 'make' readers any more efficiently than its counterpart, represented during the 1970s and 1980s as the 'real books' position. Increasing evidence from much reading research suggests that a 'balanced' approach – known more familiarly as the 'top down, bottom up' model – is the most supportive way of providing the many different sorts of knowledge most children require to become the kinds of readers our society needs. But the choice of the 'middle ground' is itself a matter of ideological positioning, and requires some background theory to establish its proper validity.

Teachers of all subjects in the secondary curriculum also need to be at least familiarised with the theories of reading for purposes of real continuity. In September 1998, the overwhelming majority of primary schools in England and Wales adopted the National Literacy Strategy Framework document as the central planning tool for teaching literacy, mostly organised within a Literacy Hour taught to all classes every day. Firmly embedded in the Literacy Framework document is a model of reading already discussed. The National Literacy Strategy team refer to this model as the Searchlights approach to reading (see Figure 1.1). This model recognises the centrality of the text, and likens the ways pupils discover meaning in the text to 'searchlights' being trained on it, illuminating the different 'knowledges' a reader has to acquire and improve.

At its introduction, because of the enormous haste of establishing it in schools, the Strategy was notably short of any published theory. It lost much good will and early ground in convincing teachers of its potential usefulness by failing to present a rationale for many of the features on which the National Literacy team originally insisted. Most of these elements, such as shared and guided reading and writing, explicit teaching and independent working, ways of learning about texts, and the plenary session were all well founded in educational reading research, but in the scramble of implementation these helpful footnotes were omitted. In fact, Roger Beard of the School of Education at the University of Leeds did publish *National Literacy Strategy: Review of Research and other Related Evidence* (Beard 1998), but it went almost unnoticed by schools then wholly absorbed in attempting to make the Literacy Framework have effect in classrooms.

As stated in the Introduction, everybody needs to be taught and to improve in at least three ways to acquire sufficient overall knowledge to be regarded as 'readers'. The first necessary reading knowledge is **semantic knowledge**, the second is **syntactic knowledge** and the third – but equally important – is **grapho-phonological knowledge**.

Semantic knowledge

Readers have to know that texts exist in the world because they are meaningful, and therefore a reader will be interested in seeking the particular meanings of particular texts. To know about texts means needing to know about the world, and the ways texts work in the world. Texts come into being for many different reasons, and represent many points of view. Readers have to learn that there are thousands of possible texts, continually expanding in number and use, and many are related to specific social, learning, professional, religious and other contexts, all with different (although sometimes related) purposes. Others have wider application. Readers have to know that certain sorts of texts are likely to move in certain, predictable directions, although a few can still surprise. As readers, we may enjoy some sorts of text in preference to others, but we may still have to refer to those – for special purposes – we do not enjoy. The really important learning many accomplished readers gradually begin to understand is that it is never possible to complete learning about reading. All readers will continue to encounter unknown texts throughout the course of their life, and each will make new demands.

Schools clearly have enormous responsibilities in helping pupils know more about more texts, about becoming 'active' readers when encountering unfamiliar texts, and in developing strategies to make the most meaning. Every teacher in the school has a role to play in this area of reading knowledge.

Syntactic knowledge

Texts are made of language. Readers have to know how our language works in different sorts of texts. The language of a fairy tale is not only, probably, simpler than the language of a chemistry textbook, but it is being deployed in a different manner (although linguistic simplicity should not be associated only with texts expressing simple ideas). The metaphors of one would be inappropriate in the other. Reading and language researchers are able to show teachers increasing evidence about how certain sorts of text can be identified from their language characteristics, and pupils need access to this knowledge.

Teachers, too, will need some assistance with their own knowledge about language as used in a variety of texts. I am not suggesting that teachers have to specifically teach language skills to their pupils, but they need to be aware of the sorts of problems language can present to readers, and be ready to address them in those circumstances.

Grapho-phonological knowledge

Readers have to be able to recognise the (usually) black printed symbol on the page, remember the sound attached to that symbol and attach it to the other symbols alongside it. Sometimes the symbol is straightforward – the short 'a' sound in 'cat', for instance – but there are many complications. A major difficulty of the English language is that it contains 26 letters, but about (only ever approximate, because dialect makes a difference) 44 sounds. So, the 'ph' of 'phonic' is said like the 'f' sound in 'fish'. While readers are recognising the 'little pictures' of each of the letters, they are also fitting sounds together in blends, and choosing the alternative sounds – is the 'c' soft, as in 'cite' or hard, as in 'clot'? This collection of miracles occurs hundreds of times a second, and is the beginning set of actions in the reading process.

For the first time in the history of the English education system it is possible to be sure that the majority of primary schools are teaching their pupils to read within broadly similar approaches. The Strategy is a mixture of different balances, all previously missing from primary literacy teaching. Before the Strategy was introduced most programmes of literacy in primary schools were 'fiction-heavy'; that is, most of the texts pupils encountered – even sometimes for finding information – were narrative fictions of one sort or another. So one of the major requirements of the Strategy was an insistence on the teaching of reading of non-fiction texts. It is becoming increasingly clear, to those who have the opportunity to monitor literacy teaching in primary schools, that far more time is being spent on deconstructing and analysing the nature of recount, procedural, non-chronological report, explanation and persuasive texts during the first 15 months of the Strategy than ever before. These developments are good grounds for persuading all teachers in secondary schools to take more notice of the nature of reading, and to concern themselves in its wider improvement.

The English curriculum

It is assumed that most secondary schools believe that the greatest, although not the whole, responsibility for the teaching of reading is ascribed to the English department. Schools have to consider this starting point, if they intend to make proper overall reading progress. Most schools will probably agree with this assertion, but the responsibility might be assigned to a cross-curricular group, even the special needs department in certain circumstances.

It is a reasonable expectation to ask an English department, before it sets out to teach reading, to address some difficult questions about what it understands to be the nature of reading, and what 'reading' means to:

- themselves, the teachers;
- their pupils;
- their pupils and their literacy needs for wider learning in school;
- their pupils and their general reading interests and pleasures;
- their pupils and their literacy needs in their lives beyond school;
- their pupils and their needs to succeed in English examinations and external examinations in other subjects.

Traves (1994), in his essay on reading, wrote:

It seems to me that there is a series of key questions that need to be addressed before we can get to grips with the teaching and learning of reading:

- What impact do we want reading to have on the lives of children we teach?
- What does it mean to be a reader?
- What is involved in the process of reading?
- What implications do these questions have for schools in general and English teachers in particular?

It should be clear to the school that the wide-ranging interests of these questions extend much further than the boundaries of the English department. The reading responsibilities of English teachers can only properly be effective, and have real authority, if they are defined and operated within the reading context of the whole school. Even the most cursory examination of 'reading' will soon suggest to all the staff of a school that pupils are constantly being asked to operate different reading practices through the range of subjects they study. Some educational researchers (Webster *et al.* 1996) would suggest that the business of schooling is wholly about the reading and the associated construction of texts:

The very nature of literacy is constituted in the wide variety of forms and functions literacy serves in different learning contexts. Put more directly, literacy is the curriculum.

The English department and reading in school

Secondary schools have to begin making realistic approaches to the literacy challenges they are increasingly recognising in their new intakes of pupils. Many are more readily accepting a larger degree of responsibility for making an improvement in those overall learning skills enabling pupils to seek improved attainment, including reading. It is no longer acceptable, nor possible, to make any progress merely by blaming the schools their pupils previously attended. As the subject called English has traditionally been regarded as the subject more obviously associated with reading, and because much of the work of English is described through specifically linguistic means, it is reasonable to begin working on the reading concerns of the school from that base. But, as the introductory comments to this chapter made clear, the English department cannot and should not be expected to tackle the whole reading programme of any school by itself. The support of a senior manager, at least at the level of the Deputy Head, responsible for curriculum and learning, is essential if this enterprise is to have any real impact on whole-school practices.

Recent history should be able to teach us a clear lesson on this matter. In the late 1970s, when most secondary schools made hesitant and preliminary attempts to implement the whole-school language and learning recommendations of the Bullock Report, those initiatives foundered in most places because Heads of English were expected to take an impossible level of responsibility relative to other departments, without senior management support. In whole-school INSET sessions I have led during the past fifteen years, there has been a regular undercurrent of resentment from teachers of other subjects (usually, but not always, scientists, I am sorry to relate) who complain that they are being expected to 'teach English'! I have to try to explain patiently, again and again, that teachers have missed the point of the exercise if that is how they depict it.

Robert Protherough (1995), who has studied and written extensively about reading in school, suggests four main topics which should occupy English teachers:

- the nature of the reading process (and more specifically the purposes of reading in school);
- the principles by which materials for reading should be selected;
- the definition of what constitutes 'progress' or 'development' in reading;
- the role of the teacher in encouraging and monitoring this progress.

One matter requiring some notice and attention at this juncture is the position regularly taken by English teachers about their reading engagements with pupils. If most English teachers are asked about the priorities they are pursuing in regard to their pupils' reading success, they are likely to give an answer which includes 'reading for pleasure' and developing the ability 'to respond' to texts (Barton 1992) because the texts they immediately think of are fictional narratives, of one sort or another.

> Most teachers of English will agree that, however much media pundits muddy the waters, our central responsibility remains what it always was: to develop in our pupils pleasure in reading, sensitivity to literature, a critical response, a sense of discrimination.

This view can be at odds with the school's own priorities. The school requires its young people to be able to make working meaning in a variety of texts, presented in a number of contexts. It wants its pupils to be independently capable of interrogating texts for a wide range of purposes. To be successful as readers across the curriculum, pupils should be skilled in making sense of different texts. They are not, within the criteria of this perspective, required to actually like the texts they read, or to have any feelings about them. If they do enjoy the texts they are reading, logic suggests they might engage with them more closely, but shared perceptions and understandings of what 'reading' means across the school have to recognise these importantly disparate perceptions.

If the English department has, after these preliminaries, been designated as the senior partner for teaching reading it will mean that the whole school has to realise the size of such an undertaking, and recognise its wider implications. Few English departments could begin putting this responsibility into practice without preparatory investment of time for training for all their staff. It is not surprising, given all the recent, externally determined priorities faced by English departments, that so few teachers have already been prepared for teaching reading. The national approach to educational change during the past two decades has also mitigated against such long-term developments, with so many piecemeal initiatives being constantly presented to teachers, liable to be to re-evaluated and amended only a short time after original implementation. (The National Curriculum can serve as a good example: the English element was introduced in 1989/90; a review was carried out through 1993/94 for introduction in 1995; the subject statutory orders were changed again in 1998/99 for introduction in 2000.)

Before deciding what would constitute an essential comprehensive reading programme capable of satisfying the needs of the whole school, any English department would have to establish which textual interactions it must and should promote within its own work. This process is by no means an easy one to fulfil. The curriculum of an English department should be the overall teaching programme guiding a group of teachers, intended to meet the pupils' linguistic and language needs, ensuring incorporation of the 'entitlement' requirements of the National Curriculum, ultimately leading to the greatest personal and academic success for all pupils. The curriculum should be capable of 'reaching backwards' to recognise the linguistic experiences encountered by the pupils in their primary schools, their personal lives and wider community, before arriving at secondary school, and 'projecting forward' to experiences likely to be encountered in the future, in and beyond the school.

Unfortunately, there is nothing 'straightforward' about pupils' linguistic experience; it can only be traced, understood and explained in relation to each and every individual pupil. This difficulty is not the only problem 'English' departments face in attempting to construct the best curriculum programme. The English language is the means of communication in our society, the medium for learning of most school subjects, and a subject in its own right. Those young people who speak English as a first language also construct their own individuality through the language. Teachers of the subject know that they can only ever touch on generalised, arbitrarily chosen areas of experience, in the hope that they have the broadest positive effects in terms of knowledge and understanding of texts for the greatest numbers of their pupils. Protherough and Atkinson (1994) point out:

> Only a small part of the teaching of English is carried out by English teachers; children arrive at the school with a wealth of existing language experience; the goals of English are not simply subject-specific ones, but are concerned with all aspects of learning and living. English teaches the abilities that underlie the learning of all other subjects. English lessons are concerned with all aspects of the individual; thoughts and feelings are inseparable; students' responses are an essential element of what is being studied; individual differences are often more significant than universal truths. Because there is no generally agreed body of subject matter, the boundaries of the subject are notoriously unclear and cannot be neatly defined.

English teachers really do need the understanding of their senior managers in facing these difficulties, and some means of sharing the questions these problems raise with all their other colleagues. Unless this wider discussion takes place, schools will continue to operate in small compartments, without ever offering their pupils a collaborative learning overview.

The nature of the reading process and the purposes of reading in school

Only a handful of English teachers have ever been taught anything about the nature of reading or the reading process. Slightly more emphasis on this area of knowledge will be a Teacher Training Agency requirement in the future training of teachers for the secondary phase from the end of the 1990s, but not much. The best common starting point of virtually every English department to prepare for teaching reading, after agreeing on principles of language learning (see page 10), would be to explore some descriptions of the reading process.

Deciding what ought to be included in the reading programme of the department has been an ongoing struggle of enormous proportions for many teachers over the past few years. English teachers are very aware of the problems of textual choice; every text which is chosen for sharing or study means that any number of other texts have been excluded from the pupils' experience for the time being.

And, as stressed earlier in this chapter, reading is not a fixed idea; it is capable of reinterpretation in different contexts. Gunther Kress, for instance, in an influential monograph developed from an address to the National Association of Advisers of English (NAAE) in 1993, advances a strong and radical argument suggesting that how we signify as individuals depends on our understanding of the nature of the texts around us. Kress (1995) proposes three sorts of text:

- the culturally salient text
- the aesthetically valued (and valuable) text
- the mundane text

as having specific functions in the curriculum. Because he is exploring an inevitably growing multicultural dimension to the English curriculum, the 'culturally salient' criterion asks 'what significance does this text have in its own cultural domain?' This shift, Kress claims, 'from aesthetic concerns to those of salience, proves essential and liberating, not just within the curriculum but within broader cultural politics.' This reference has not been included to baffle teachers even more, merely to indicate that any decisions taken about reading and which texts to study can never be an absolute; all choices and categories of reading are wholly arbitrary.

An exercise undertaken with some Heads of English departments is salutary, re-emphasising how necessary some form of theory is to establishing an effective, influential reading programme likely to support their pupils. I ask my colleagues to calculate how many hours of English their pupils might be timetabled during the whole of Key Stage 3. It is unlikely to be many more than 350 hours. I then ask them to 'brainstorm' all the sorts of texts they could think of. The list quickly becomes enormous! The next stage is to select all the texts the English team believes should be included in a fully developed English curriculum for pupils aged 11–14 (ensuring, of course, that the requirements of the National Curriculum have been satisfactorily met). Each form of selected text could only be considered for a few hours of possible study. Those taking part in this exercise are then asked to consider all the texts left over in their list, and to assign appropriate examples to other departments. It still leaves a great many texts unaccounted for, and unlikely to be taught by anybody.

That little task is of itself very superficial, but has a powerful effect in raising the obvious questions of curriculum inclusion. Asking marginally more detailed questions soon presents enormous difficulties related to choice of texts for the classroom. One of the forms chosen for study is bound to be 'the novel'. What sort of novel ought to be studied in the classroom and at what points during the Key Stage? In schools where there are a number of capable readers, making their own choices of texts to be read independently beyond the classroom, there will also be Year 7 pupils reading Enid Blyton, Roald Dahl, or books from the 'Babysitter' or 'Goosebumps' series. Are these novels worthy or demanding of study in English lessons? If not, why not? They are, after all, selections pupils are making for themselves, and we know enough about reading to recognise that young people read more enthusiastically if the texts engage their attention immediately.

The last two decades have seen an explosion of very fine writers publishing novels for young adults. Philip Pullman, Peter Dickinson, Malorie Blackman, Anne Fine, Robert Swindells and David Almond are names which spring immediately to mind. These novelists are continually publishing new works, against the background of a huge canon of publications already available. Should the texts of these writers be regarded as the necessary content of the Key Stage 3 reading curriculum? They are dealing with contemporary subjects and issues, which we know have immediate obvious appeal to young adolescent readers. The school is the proper setting for children to be put into contact with materials they would be unlikely to stumble on without assistance. Should the English department include some of these works in their reading programme (and if so, which should they choose?.)

Having agreed that the department will maintain a wholly contemporary reading curriculum, how will the teachers help pupils to become acquainted with a group of writers whose work is now some 30 or more years old? Do we then neglect and forget works by Rosemary Sutcliffe, Leon Garfield, C. S. Lewis and Alan Garner, to name a few? Or, just to complicate matters a little more, perhaps these novelists move after a few years into another category known as 'significant children's authors', which is a compulsory area of study in Key Stage 2! At Key Stages 3 and 4 the amended curriculum, published in 1999, insists that pupils must read 'two works of fiction of high quality by major authors published before 1914'. There is also an imperative that pupils' reading must include 'two works of fiction of high quality by major writers with well-established critical reputations, whose works were published after 1914.' Each one of these epithets – 'high-quality', 'major', 'well-established critical reputations' – merely raises more questions than it answers.

To establish some sort of control and sensible rationale for reading in the face of the statutory requirements, and balancing these against the reading 'needs' of the pupils, firmly emphasises the need for a guiding policy. Every English department should be able to make a clear explanation of why particular texts, or sorts of texts, have been chosen, to themselves, their colleagues in the school, external agencies interested in their work, their parents and their pupils. Having made their decisions and articulated them, members of the department should be prepared to be challenged by any of those named groups, and be ready to engage in the healthy discourses those challenges could present.

It is not my intention to instruct any department about the materials it should choose to buy and use for teaching purposes. However, teachers ought to review carefully the ways texts are selected for different groups. They should make choices based on:

- the interests of their pupils;
- the likelihood of positive engagement;
- the provision of the necessary statutory range;
- the potential *learning* these texts could promote.

Teachers designing the curriculum of the English department will need to have considered where the subject **English** stands in relation to the **literacy** programme of the school, which will include whole-staff attitudes to reading, writing, speaking and listening in all lessons through the school. Relating their own linguistic responsibilities against a broader whole-school literacy context should trigger important discussions and considerations about reading in every school, in which the English teachers will be playing a major part.

Chapter 4

Qualities and Characteristics of the Reader and Assessing Reading Improvement

> The most fundamental aspects of learning to read are not about skills; they are about learning to behave like a reader. (Harrison and Coles 1992)

Teachers intending to teach reading and to improve the reading attainment of their pupils are more likely to succeed if they have already determined for themselves some characteristics which define a reader. Their teaching will then be more likely to enhance the features they have identified. It may seem unusual that any group of professionals can embark on a programme of improving something, without quite knowing what it is that they will bring about through that process. Yet, to a great extent, that is what has been happening in the teaching of reading within English studies. My caricature might be thought a little harsh, but when asked the direct question, 'How would your department describe a reader?' Heads of English reach for some strange, and sometimes unrelated, criteria. The colleague who looked for: 'those pupils who can make out the words, then those who can make literal sense, and – at the top of the scale – those who can read between the lines,' at least based his description on a progressive scale, but it revealed few areas of potential growth worth developing.

This is a topic lacking any real precision. A 'reader', as argued in the Introduction, can mean many things in different circumstances. With the gradual introduction of greater accountability relating to their work, huge numbers of English teachers have become suspicious of what they regard as the 'mechanisation' of their subject. They dislike and disown an increasing growth of a vocabulary more in keeping with industrial manufacturing, such as 'outcomes' and 'products'. They claim that the intrinsic nature of the subject is about tuning sensitively to the linguistic needs and understanding of individual pupils, and encouraging language growth through increasingly critical encounters with texts. The trend of the last few years, with insistence on league tables, target setting and other trappings of control and measurable results, is at odds with the potential individual growth of each pupil, so important to English teachers.

But, inescapably, schools have to be able to demonstrate *how* they are making a positive difference to pupils' achievements. They have to be able to identify for themselves, their pupils, parents, external monitoring agencies and their communities the priority areas of learning, experience and awareness they wish their young people to take away with them after 11 years of compulsory education. Reading is so central to all those discussions that its nurturing and development cannot be left to chance. It is also an area of teaching and learning responsibility belonging to a much wider group of teachers than the English team, and therefore any criteria about reading directing the work of the English teachers have to be fully aligned with the ways of working of their colleagues.

Therefore, before the school, or the English department pioneering this work on behalf of the school, begins actually to devise a deliberate programme to teach reading, there ought to be a universal agreement of what that institution believes a reader to be.

The following are some suggested qualities or attributes which, together, might be thought of as defining and identifying a reader. I do not claim that they have any status beyond the help they provided when I was trying to establish a real focus for planning with primary schools attempting to give sense to the mass of unwieldy teaching objectives which comprise the National Literacy Strategy Framework folder. Although the Framework document is full of excellent objectives, designed to contribute to the provision of a comprehensive language and literacy curriculum in the primary years, it is possible to select objectives for planning from Reception to Year 6 without making much coherent development in the pupils' linguistic attainment. Rather than choosing apparently related word level, sentence level and text level objectives in a term by term collection, for their own sake – as many schools were – I wanted to assist teachers in focusing their teaching to more clearly distinguished and articulated learning goals. In discussion with several primary English co-ordinators, we gradually identified a series of central principles or strands about reading, writing, speaking and listening to which we could apply the objectives.

These principles or qualities are all capable of being separated into progressive stages or steps. They are all possible to improve, but no learner will ever 'conquer' any of them. There will always be something new to achieve, and continuing life experiences mean that every reader will discover more about reading than would have previously been known. The team realised that the central core of reading qualities we had identified did not solely apply to one phase of education. They can be used for all readers at whatever stage of development they have reached, so these same qualities would be just as appropriate for describing readers in a nursery class as they would be for A level students in the sixth form.

Teachers accepting these qualities as realistic strands of possible reading development should then be able to plan any reading work they intend with their classes as contributing to one or more of these qualities through all Key

Stages. Policies for reading will be more firmly based on principles, not merely plucked from the air. Pupils made aware of them could be urged to use these descriptors and their increasing understanding of them as starting points for their own self-assessment. Of course, what pupils actually learn about reading could well turn out to be more than has been planned for in this approach. Teachers are aware that pupils are always likely to take from their reading experiences more than was originally planned. But they will not in any way be disadvantaged by the adoption of a 'spine' of core descriptive elements relating to the reader that should give greater cohesion to any reading programme. Agreement about these reading qualities by teachers in different phases of education should also make liaison about the reading curriculum easier between schools dealing with primary and secondary aged pupils.

These qualities of a reader are one suggested way of helping to identify necessary areas of teaching. They provide a means of breaking through some of the reserve often expressed about teaching reading, and they point to a more practical, focused approach. They are not the only way this objective might be pursued. I urge English departments and schools to come up with their own principles on which they could base their own work, if these suggestions do not meet their immediate needs. But it is important to establish a clearer and more collaborative view that enables all teachers to feel that they have a more realistic stake in the reading development of their pupils. They need to have an agenda through which they are better able to plan and describe the improvements that everybody outside school expects them to bring about.

These qualities are founded on wide-ranging research into reading, and recognise the breadth of the reading process. They are not conveyed in any particular order of importance, although most teachers would probably agree that the first point is the best place to start.

Twelve qualities of a reader

The qualities that were identified by the team are first listed, and then each one will be considered in more detail.

This school/department believes that:

1. a reader knows that reading is a complex, intellectual endeavour, requiring the reader to draw on a range of active meaning-making skills;
2. a reader deploys previous knowledge of other texts to enable the effective reading and further meaning-making of the text being read;
3. a reader is aware that texts are constructed for particular purposes, for identifiable audiences and within recognisable text types or genres;
4. a reader can predict the ways that texts work, and can use reading to confirm or readjust those predictions, depending on how typically the text unfolds;

5. a reader is critically active before becoming involved in the substantial body of any text;
6. a reader is increasingly able to activate a repertoire of critical questions in engagements with new and unfamiliar texts;
7. a reader knows how to interact appropriately with a variety of text types / genres for particular purposes;
8. a reader is aware that one way of demonstrating progression in reading can be through raising more complex questions about the same text;
9. a reader is aware that learning to read is a life-long continuous process;
10. a reader is aware that all readers do not necessarily read and make meanings in the same ways as one another;
11. a reader will be able to explain why a text has been rejected, unfinished, or how it has been unable to satisfy the tasks to which it was put;
12. a reader improves when encouraged and taught to monitor and reflect on own reading ability and progress.

What do these twelve reading qualities mean in practice?

1. A reader knows that reading is a complex, intellectual endeavour, requiring a range of active meaning-making skills

Pupils have to be aware that reading is much more than the process of decoding. To read properly means calling on a whole repertoire of preliminary preparatory competencies. Reading researchers describe this knowledge as the ability to 'interrogate' a text; to ask questions of it. Poor readers do not know that they have to work hard to make the text come alive. The reader has to attempt to 'place' the text relative to the total extent of all other known texts before all the reader's meaning-making capabilities can be deployed.

As discussed on page 63 a good reader attaches the sounds to the symbols of the letters comprising each word being read (word level), while analysing the function of that word in relation to the words surrounding it (sentence level), relating those perceptions within a knowledge of whole texts (text level); all in the tiniest fraction of a second! Teaching of reading should be addressing these three levels of 'readerly' behaviour, to make them completely integrated and seamless in the reader's toolkit. We see and hear too many young people in their early teens unable to activate each of these skills in isolation, let alone simultaneously calling on all of them together.

2. A reader draws on previous knowledge of other texts to enable the effective reading and further meaning-making of the text being read

All readers are the amalgam of all their previous textual encounters. The greater their experiences, the more the background knowledge on which they can call, and apply to their new textual engagements. Of course, not all the texts a reader calls on will be reading texts, or published in print on a page. Young readers might well have seen a cartoon animation of a story similar to the one now being read, or vice versa, and they might be using the narrative structure of one media form to help make greater meaning of the other. When assisting less confident readers to make meaning in their hesitant attempts, it is usual to make reference to other, better known sources likely to deal with related ideas. Many contemporary advertisements rely on our previous knowledge of phrases, words or images from elsewhere, and some animated series, such as *The Simpsons*, wholly depend on this 'intertextual' relationship.

When a reader discovers a 'favourite' author, she or he is likely to select further texts by that writer, because the reader expects particular pleasures or experiences from the initial contact to be repeated. Adults and children regularly seek for more examples of admired 'starter texts'.

Nearly every child begins its reading experiences with narrative fiction texts. As pupils pass through the different phases of education, they encounter an increasing range of texts, many of them quite unrelated to their first experiences. They continually need further assistance in studying the particular characteristics of each of these texts, to build an increasing repertoire of textual knowledge.

3. A reader is aware that texts are constructed for particular purposes, for identifiable audiences, within recognisable text types/genres

This knowledge is equally important in teaching and learning about writing as it is for teaching and learning about reading. In most circumstances in the real world, unlike some which take place in school, texts are deliberate constructs to serve real purposes. They come about because a writer has something significant to express. The most effective way of making that expression is in a textual form which will be familiar to the intended audience, in a style that the audience will think of as appropriate. Sometimes, of course, the text maker might want to challenge the parameters of certain sorts of text, in which case the readers will need to know which parameters are being challenged to have a real sense of what is being attempted!

Readers need to 'place' themselves in relation to the text. They need to be able to 'hear' the writer, to tune to the nuances, rhythms and patterns of the text before they can gain sufficient purchase to pursue further meaning. (Listen to a range of Year 9 pupils with different reading attainments attempting their first speaking out loud of Shakespeare's dramatic poetry! This is not a cheap aside; the Key Stage 3 English tests employ this form of text to assess the reading of all 14-year-old pupils in England.)

They need to be aware of how language is expected to work in particular circumstances to make its effects. Good readers are aware of the relationship between style, structure and meaning. Those who struggle with reading are not able to involve themselves as closely in the movement or pace of the text at an early enough stage to recognise how it can contribute to the way it ought to be interpreted.

While all fictional stories might look, superficially, the same, there are obvious differences between most fictional texts and many texts written for information. Textbooks in different subjects often resemble each other in a number of respects, but the aware reader will be looking out for the ways in which they deviate. Information might be conveyed through straightforward instruction; through raising issues and comparing them; through the presentation of some evidence calling on the active drawing together of those strands by the reader. Knowing how the information has been presented will make the use and interpretation of that information much easier to discover for whoever is seeking it.

4. *A reader can predict the ways that texts work, and can use reading to confirm or readjust those predictions, depending on how typically the text unfolds*

A reader will become involved more quickly in a text if its structure is already familiar. Most obviously, a poem usually differs in structure from a narrative fiction. The potential reader of the poem will already be prepared for the demands the text is likely to make before reading in earnest. Many narrative fictions develop along chronological lines. When these orderings of times are tampered with, or disturbed, the reader becomes used to looking out for clues to the changes. The next time the developing reader encounters a narrative fiction, there will already be an expectation that not all the time orderings need to be chronological.

Practised readers become more and more confident about slipping into the 'routines' of books, but they know that those 'routines' have to be searched out at an early stage of the engagement. Texts often surprise. Indeed, many readers enjoy pursuing their reading to discover these surprises. Occasionally, however, readers like to settle into familiar patterns. Experienced adult readers will enjoy the stories of Sherlock Holmes, or the novels of Ruth Rendell, precisely because there are patterns and routines which will reassure them and contribute to the way that the story might relax the reader. Pupils have their own favourites of texts offering familiar routines: Enid Blyton became a children's favourite because her readers discovered and became comfortable with the 'formula' of her structuring; the Harry Potter novels are a more recent example of this same phenomenon.

5. *A reader is critically active before becoming involved in the substantial body of any text*

A reader has usually selected a text, or is in the process of selecting a text, for a particular and known reason. In schools, pupils occasionally find texts placed before them for reasons which have not always been shared with them! Usually, however, the reader has a fairly clear idea why the text is being read. This means that there are already expectations about what the text is likely to yield before the first page is tackled.

Even when readers encounter unfamiliar texts, they are able to begin 'framing' their perceptions before the full engagement of reading begins. There might be some direct questions: is this a work of fiction or non-fiction?; are the expressions I am about to read likely to be opinion or fact?; do I know other examples of this author's work, or anything about that person?; what is the cover, the layout, the font, the use of illustrations telling me about this text?

Probably every English teacher poses a series of preparatory questions to all their classes before beginning class 'readers' or any other text, and they will expect the pupils to be more prepared for the subsequent exploration as a result. But while that practice may be common in the English classroom, it is a process almost never used as preparation of texts in other subjects. Most teachers have simply never considered that the skill of raising questions about the texts supporting the subject could be a useful way of aligning the reader to the way the text works.

6. *A reader is increasingly able to activate a repertoire of critical questions in engagements with new and unfamiliar texts*

This quality develops from the previous one. Through practising the process of raising appropriate questions about familiar texts, readers will be expected to become increasingly confident about engaging with those new to them. Many poor readers turn their backs on texts they perceive as presenting nothing but obstacles, and lack resources enabling them to gain a sufficient purchase on the text to make real progress. Urged 'to have a go' they regularly become more and more recalcitrant, afraid that their efforts will amuse or anger others and continue to confirm their own lack of self-belief.

It is essential that pupils become more confident about tackling unfamiliar material; some might claim that this preparation of young people for the future should be the central concern of the contemporary English curriculum. As our technologies inevitably multiply, and they come to play a more significant part in our everyday lives, people are likely to encounter and be expected to know their way round even more textual material. We have, currently, few resources and little vision in schools to enable pupils to grow and develop in these future demands.

7. *A reader knows how to interact appropriately with a variety of text types/genres for particular purposes*

Different sorts of texts require different reading strategies. Readers usually make their way, chronologically, stage by stage through fictional narratives (although a few people always read the ending first). They will be more likely to skim across a piece of informational text, seeking the particular reference they require. The vocabulary of some texts is more likely to enable a smooth, connected, coherent reading experience, whereas the language of others causes the reader to stop, reread, check back to previous references or distinguish each word carefully. Sometimes the reading experience might mean 'losing' oneself in the text, while on other occasions the reader has to stand at a distance from the textual material, asking questions about the possible source or motive of the material being considered.

Pupils have to realise that the whole meaning of texts will not always be immediately available, even for supposedly 'good' readers. Many texts require the reader to 'fill in the gaps', to use the given information to infer or deduce further features not spelled out. Sometimes the reader might have to work out that there has been a switching of time in the text, or that the true nature of certain characters can be worked out from their actions, in direct contravention of what they claim about themselves.

Teachers of subjects other than English are not usually aware that texts differ so considerably from subject to subject. Or that readers treat texts differently for different purposes. Kress (1991), among others, describes these textual differences as the 'institutional discourses' of separate 'social domains':

> Discourses are important in schools, particularly in secondary schools and tertiary education, because the organisation of knowledge becomes more and more specific to the disciplines which a child or student enters into. Thus you have particular ways of writing which correspond to the ways of organising knowledge within a particular discipline. As you move from primary to secondary the two categories, the forms in which writing appears and the forms in which knowledge about a particular domain is represented, become more and more important and so the emphasis in writing shifts from mechanical things and learning the new conventions of the mode of writing, to the problems of coping with understanding the forms of the texts, the genres which are specific to school and the organisation of knowledge.

8. *A reader is aware that one way of demonstrating progress in reading can be through raising more complex questions about the same text*

Too often, parents and teachers are inclined to think of pupils making progress only if they appear to be moving through stages of apparently more difficult texts. The whole 'reading scheme' ethos lends itself to and promotes this sort of assessment. Young pupils, invited to describe themselves as readers have been heard to respond, 'I'm on Orange!', meaning that they have reached a certain stage of difficulty not made clear to themselves, but assumed through the school. Or, comparing themselves with others in the class, a children might describe classmates in terms of the stages they have attained: 'I'm a better reader than whoever, because he's only on level 4!'

Publishers regularly advertise new ranges of texts for less confident readers, especially boys, by making claims about the simplicity of the language. These books, usually on topics or about figures more likely to appeal to boys, are presented as vehicles for helping reluctant readers back to mainstream reading habits. I contend that attempting to write books for adolescent boys in undemanding language misses the real point. These lads will not be convinced that they are being denied the important experience of reading through only encountering a level of language unable to excite or stimulate their dormant interest. They will not discover the remedy to their problems through consuming as many of these books as possible! Enormous quantities of this level of text are to be found on the shelves of Special Needs departments in secondary schools – mostly untouched. Readers are not made by presenting struggling pupils with edited or abridged versions of classic texts either. They could probably follow a complex plot line by this means, but they will not be any closer to understanding why accomplished readers regard such texts as worthwhile.

A good reader will be able to read the same text at different stages through his or her life and know that there are more and more questions to ask, and issues to raise, at each stage. A small child at an early stage of reading development might discover Anthony Browne's picture text *The Tunnel* (1989), and enjoy the story of the modest, unadventurous little girl who, through an enormous act of courage, rescues and restores her much more outgoing brother from an act of incaution. At a later stage, the developing reader will look more carefully at the visual and verbal devices Browne employs to establish the relationship between the two siblings. More accomplished, the reader might recognise levels of symbolism in the story and make broader interpretations of what the characters represent. As an undergraduate, the reader could look again at the book and muse about the important psychological aspects of human nature explored in the text. At parents' evenings in schools to demonstrate the nature of reading, I am often asked about the appropriate age group for a particular book. I usually reply by illustrating the range of activities possible to interest the reader of that text aged six, then aged nine, and then aged 14.

Knowing a text contains meaning requires readers to seek for that meaning. Some more challenging works may well have further layers of meaning, and good readers realise that rereading will allow them to discover more than might have been discovered on first acquaintance (Watson 1993):

> What is a multi-layered text?... it is any text which on subsequent readings yields more pleasure, more significance, and enables the reader to experience a growing sense of delighted understanding and familiarity. When we re-read a complex text we get better at it; so a multi-layered text is one which invites a reader to become more skilled at reading it.

Effective teaching of reading will want to urge pupils to realise that what might be discovered in an initial reading is not necessarily all there is. Learning about this area of reading will be evidenced when pupils automatically want to re-engage with texts, confident that they will find more to take away from them.

9. A reader is aware that learning to read is a life-long continuous process

We never complete the task of learning to read. It would be impossible to make automatic meaning from every text we might encounter, because there are far too many texts to know, and new texts continue to come into existence day by day. Teachers, as part of the reading process, will want their pupils to recognise the extent of their knowledge about texts, and to reflect on what more they might need to find out about those areas of reading in which they might be less fluent or accomplished. Readers might think themselves comfortable and familiar with certain texts, believing that they have discovered the possible meanings contained within them, only to engage in other experiences or to gain further insights which increase their knowledge even further.

10. A reader is aware that all readers do not necessarily read and make meaning in the same ways as one another

We all bring different life and textual experiences to texts. We bring different reading backgrounds to texts, and texts play different parts in all our lives. Depending on our own cultural pasts, texts will yield many possible ranges of meaning, unique to each of us.

Griffith (1987) first quotes Barthes: 'Any text is a new tissue of past citations. Bits of code, formulae, rhythmic models, fragments of social languages, etc. pass into the text and are redistributed within it, for there is always language before and around the text', before going on to state:

> With such a complex artefact, varying readings are not only possible, they are positively obligatory.... There is no central core of meaning to be discovered.

The growing readers in our schools need to realise that they do not have to see the same meanings in their reading matter as other pupils in their class, or their teacher. They have to develop the confidence to show how a passage or a whole text conjures up ways of interpretation not obviously contained within the text itself. Through realising that their own 'readings' have validity, not dependent on the suggestions of others, pupils should discover more resources for engaging with texts more closely. Watson (1993) quotes a story about a Year 6 boy rereading John Burningham's *Granpa*, who explained:

> ...without apparent embarrassment that the book made him feel like crying
> – though he had read it in an infant class without being upset by it – and he

knew that this was because a much-loved member of the family had recently died. This young reader knew about death and grief; and he also saw – and talked about – the connection between his life and his reading.

11. A reader will be able to explain why a text has been rejected, unfinished, or how it has been unable to satisfy the tasks to which it was put

Not all readers will enjoy, find satisfaction in or feel the need to proceed with every text they pick up. In discovering the sorts of texts they will go on to read independently, every reader will make a number of 'mistakes' or encounter genres which give little pleasure. We all need to build up our own lists of preferred reading from a huge supply of possible titles and types of books, and will only discover just what we do enjoy – or sometimes will need – by keeping an open mind about engaging with new material. Schools are keenly aware that one of their duties is to introduce pupils to the widest possible range of texts.

Yet readers will decide that there are texts they will not want to continue reading. Schools should also be concerned with helping pupils offer reasons for not continuing with a text. Peter Traves, now a head teacher in Shropshire, but for many years an LEA English Adviser and researcher into reading, regularly stresses the *control* schools should help their pupils discover. The 'control' of choosing books to read because they know something about them and want to read them. Conversely, there is a 'control' pupils should be able to demonstrate in stepping away from a text because it does not fulfil expectations, or come up to requirements. Pupils do not have 'control' when they are unable to proceed with a text because they are already finding it difficult to make meaning of the parts, or they are unable to effect a purchase on what it might be about. To cover up this disability, young people will often 'blame' the text: 'that was boring.'

12. A reader will improve when encouraged and taught to monitor and reflect on own reading ability

The little girl responding, 'I'm on Orange!' mentioned in point 8 of this list, was someone who had not learned to evaluate her own reading abilities and needs. The English educational system has often claimed that pupils gain considerable benefit by making realistic appraisal of their own progress, but it has been poor in actually tutoring pupils in those skills. The 'plenary' session of The Literacy Hour, now current in all primary classrooms, has – not surprisingly – been one of the most difficult parts to implement. Teachers are not familiar with the demands of such a session from their own experiences and backgrounds, and they therefore find it difficult to model the required learning behaviour for their pupils.

Reading policies based on qualities of reading

Through the furthering and development of the qualities of reading explained in the preceding section of this chapter, an English department or a whole school staff would then be in a more confident position to state the following aims as matters of policy:

This department or school aims to enable pupils to:

- read fluently and with understanding across a range of texts;
- use all available clues in texts to search for meaning;
- recognise that makers of texts devise them for a variety of purposes and audiences;
- develop a range of reading strategies for individual texts, and across a range of texts;
- read for different purposes (e.g. for pleasure, to find information, to discover models for own writing, to explore the views and attitudes of others etc.);
- make realistic predictions of texts, and to check/amend those predictions depending on textual development;
- to make progress as readers;
- to become increasingly reflective on their own reading development.

Most schools will probably want to express some general expectations of all staff in their policy documentation to supplement the above aims. Statements such as:

- all teachers who include the study of text in their subjects are teachers of reading;
- readers will be assisted to improve their reading in an environment which pays attention to language;
- all departments should consider the contents, use and effectiveness of the library as a study centre as their responsibility;
- all departments should monitor and assess the reading capabilities of their pupils;

are the sorts of challenges to the teaching staff and senior management which demand full discussion, understanding and agreement in practical terms.

Assessment of reading

All contemporary research about assessment tells teachers that the most worthwhile teaching has to be based on knowing what pupils can do, and, from that knowledge, extrapolating what they need to know and be able to perform in the near future. All teachers of reading should be aware of the work of Black and Wiliam (1998), researching 'formative assessment' at Kings College, London.

Their reviews of many studies show that: 'innovations which include strengthening the practice of formative assessment produce significant, and often substantial, learning gains'. They describe 'formative assessment' thus:

> ...the term 'assessment' refers to all those activities undertaken by teachers, *and their students in assessing themselves*, which provide information to be used as feedback to modify the teaching and learning activities in which they are engaged. *Such assessment becomes 'formative assessment' when the evidence is actually used to adapt the teaching work to meet the needs.* (their italics)

Low-attainers, particularly, made considerable gains when their learning was attuned to the practices of formative assessment, and the gap between levels of attainment was seen to close.

The *First Steps* literacy programme, researched in primary schools and first published in Australia in the late 1980s, makes this statement (Pemberton and Davidson 1999):

> Assessment is the process of collecting data in order to understand the knowledge, skills and strategies that children have developed in their learning. It is integral to the teaching and learning of reading and writing because it forms the basis on which teachers
>
> • make judgements about children's learning
> • provide information about the progress of the individual
> • make decisions about instructional programmes.
>
> Assessment is also used to help pupils take ownership and control over their own learning.

The principles, in this programme, are explicitly claimed to be as true for reading as for any other area of the curriculum. Planning for learning has to satisfy the requirements of 'entitlement', as described in the English subject orders, but it should also be guided by the sensitive discovery of what pupils have already attained, and designed to make realistic forecasts of what they might be capable of attaining. Most reading activities are not planned on such solid grounds; they take place regardless of what the pupils have achieved, and the results they produce are not often carefully sought.

The ways in which reading achievement is tested and evaluated in schools will greatly influence what is taught and the sorts of reading skills that are valued and learned. Yet assessment of reading is a very variable activity in schools across the country. At the most elementary level, all schools are expected to assess their pupils at the end of Key Stage 3, relative to Level Descriptions which accompany the English subject Statutory Orders. These Level Descriptions have been devised to offer a 'best fit' snapshot of pupils' abilities at the end of Years 2, 6 and 9. The expectation of most pupils aged 14, at the end of Key Stage 3, is that they should achieve Level 5, by demonstrating the following characteristics (DFE 1995):

> Pupils show understanding of a range of texts, selecting essential points and using inference and deduction where appropriate. In their responses, they identify key features, themes and characters, and select sentences, phrases and relevant information to support their views. They retrieve and collate information from a range of sources.

Most English teachers agree that these less than specific guidelines do not lend themselves to providing accurate or supportive knowledge of what pupils are capable of doing with texts.

On the other hand, the adoption of the descriptions of qualities of a reader, outlined above, to guide planning and learning of reading would be more likely to encourage an English department team or, even better, the whole school staff into reconsidering ways of assessing their pupils. Each of the descriptive statements has the potential for offering a criterion for making judgements about pupils' reading development. So, by selecting one description against which to judge a reader (for example, 5, *A reader is critically active before becoming involved in the substantial body of any text*) teachers would want to know how adept that pupil has become in raising a whole repertoire of questions, to enable a confident engagement with a broad range of texts. Is the pupil, perhaps, able to ask a number of generic questions suitable to begin a worthwhile involvement with any sort of text, or capable of pursuing more specialist issues leading to closer reading of specific genres or text types? The limited space in this book does not allow me to explore the levels of detail in relation to each of the reader descriptions, but at a simple working level teachers would be able to devise at least a four point scale:

1. Pupils not able to raise questions about a text before reading.
2. Pupils able to raise a limited number of questions about a text before reading.
3. Pupils able to raise quite a number of questions about a text before reading.
4. Pupils capable of raising considerable numbers of questions about a text before reading.

If a teacher is aware of a group of pupils not very skilled at raising possible questions to put to an unfamiliar text, as a way of helping them make some meaning from it, then there is clearly a need to teach that skill. Those pupils able to ask just a few questions need tuition to enable them to learn more ways of opening up the text. The Russian psychologist Vygotsky (1986) illustrates how, by knowing where a pupil might be placed along a continuum, it is possible to both predict and then 'support' (or 'scaffold') that pupil to the next stage.

Secondary teachers, looking for ways to assess reading more effectively, would be greatly assisted by considering the approach adopted by the *First Steps* programme (Pemberton and Davidson 1999), which has a number of important features:

- pupils' language progression is seen as a 'continuum', beginning from the very earliest stages of language acquisition, and continuing throughout their lives;
- where a pupil is placed along that continuum is not dependent on age, or Key Stage, but on a range of attainment criteria in a particular linguistic area, such as reading/writing etc;
- pupils are differentiated, according to a range of attainment criteria, into Developmental Phases; pupils can be assisted in reaching the next Developmental Phase by being taught a clearly defined range of skills at the appropriate level of challenge ('scaffolded' in the terms of the psychologist, Vygotsky);
- it is likely that there will be groups of pupils at a number of different Developmental Phases in each classroom;
- pupils are expected to play a vital part in their own assessment.

This programme is very challenging for secondary schools. It points to the need for teachers to think of their pupils in different phases of development (*First Steps* calls each of the 'phases' of reading: 'Role Play Reading', 'Experimental Reading', 'Early Reading', 'Transitional Reading', 'Independent Reading' and 'Advanced Reading') with the obvious suggestion that, with proper support, readers can move to a more advanced phase. In any class there will be groups of pupils at different stages, with their own learning needs. The programme demands that pupils are assessed across a range of reading criteria; considering a few superficial qualities will not provide sufficient material on which to build suitable or appropriate teaching and learning. It expects teachers to have a notion of progression, understandable to all the staff and shared with the pupils. Assessment of a linguistic 'element', such as reading, depends on more evidence than can be provided through merely writing tasks.

Bearne (1998) suggests a similar approach to thinking of reading progression in relation to individuals and groups. Her book, intended for primary teachers, suggests a 'scale of progression' for readers at different stages:

A reader in the early stages of learning
A reader who is gaining experience and fluency
A more assured reader, growing in experience
A more experienced and independent reader
An experienced and almost independent reader
A very experienced and independent reader.

Once again, teachers will realise that there is a strong likelihood of pupils at different stages of reading development in every class of Key Stage 3, particularly in English departments grouping pupils by mixed ability. Bearne's 'indicators' are not as detailed as those in the *First Steps*, and might be a better starting point for teachers not so familiar with this model of assessment. They are, however, still far-ranging, covering areas of language at word, sentence and whole text levels, but they 'also go further to include the process of developing discrimination and assurance'. This notion of assessment also expects teachers to discover how well pupils demonstrate their reading learning in more ways than written tests, or log books.

Teachers do not have to be reminded how difficult it is to assess reading satisfactorily; English staff wrestle with its problems on a daily basis. Harrison (1995) wrote the following:

> It is extraordinarily difficult to get very close to a person's response to what they read. Taken further, this assertion will lead to another: that it is extraordinarily difficult to make a very satisfactory job of assessing a person's ability in reading.

But this problem does not mean we can give up trying to find a supportive way of thinking of pupils' progress. There are models of assessing reading available, which, when combined with the criteria provided by, for instance, the descriptive qualities of a reader, could allow us to make more significant judgements about the reading progress of pupils.

There are two more practical assessment activities to add to the theoretical material discussed above. Both have been successfully tested in a number of settings, with resulting improvements in teacher assessment.

Mind map of a reader

This form of asking pupils about their reading progress answers some of the problems described earlier, but it cannot offer a comprehensive assessment. Pupils are given a sheet laid out like Figure 4.1 and they place another sheet over the top, on which they make their own responses, filling in their own names in the middle. Teachers can add or omit categories as they choose. The pupils are asked to make a short response to each of the questions, not full sentences, but just a few words. They find the process easy, and are quite happy to spend a few minutes filling it out.

Teachers might ask the new intake to the school to attempt this 'test' in their first week. The sheet could then be offered for a further set of responses (with the same questions) at the end of the first half term. It could be applied again at Christmas, then at the February half term, and so on. Kept in a plastic wallet, each set of responses could be used to build up a profile of the reader. Teachers could then review the sheets on a regular basis, looking for evidence

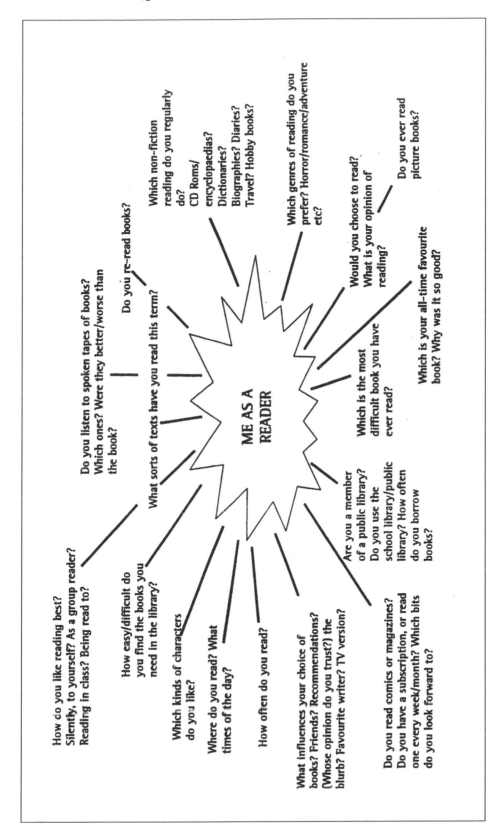

Figure 4.1 Mind map of the reader (Thanks to Jeanette Mackie, Lord William's School, Thame)

of reading growth across a number of criteria. If they do not detect pupils making much progress, they should then intervene to discover how that growth could be restored. It should also be clear that the sheet encourages readers to reflect on their reading practices and perceptions of themselves as readers. Once again, if teachers feel these self-evaluations do not accord with their own judgements, there would be an opportunity for a personal conversation about reading.

Reading interviews

My belief is that every pupil has an entitlement to at least one reading interview a year, and certainly more where schools are able to conduct them. As Harrison pointed out, in the development of the quotation included on page 76, the reading interview is probably the most accurate form of reading assessment (although even the interview can depend on the pupil's oral skills!). Interviews do not have to be conducted by teachers: I have seen successful and worthwhile interviewing by librarians, learning support assistants, sixth form students and parents. But they do need some preparation to yield appropriate information about pupils. Interviewees will be helped by preparing their thoughts about what sorts of texts they will be talking about, their reading habits and practices, their reactions to certain material and their reading biographies, among other topics. It is not necessary to interview pupils individually: two, even three, pupils at a time could discuss their reading with a single interviewer. Inter-viewees respond best if not confronted by a barrage of questions, but through being invited into the interview process by questions prefaced with phrases, such as 'Tell me about the...' 'Tell me how...' as described by Chambers (1993). Although this book was originally written to guide primary teachers in their interaction with pupils, the lessons are equally applicable to secondary colleagues.

Conclusion

Development of reading practices in secondary schools has not made much progress during the past decade. Schools should urge their staff to agree on suitable, wide-ranging criteria describing what they understand 'readers' to be. With this guiding framework it is then possible to ascertain how well they believe their pupils are performing within each of the identified categories. These judgements will be more than tick box records, they will be the next stage of the planning of teaching reading, so each school can genuinely claim their pupils are continually improving.

Chapter 5

Teaching Reading in the Secondary School

Since the pupils who have had the least success at reading are often boys, and since few secondary teachers have anything beyond the foggiest notion about how to teach reading other than to bring pupils and books into close proximity, the wonder is that there are so many successes rather than that there are such low standards of attainment. (Reynolds 1995)

The adoption of a structure, such as the descriptions of the qualities of a reader outlined in Chapter 4, makes it possible to establish some important starting points for teaching. If a reader is expected to know that reading is a complex, intellectual endeavour, requiring a range of active meaning-making skills, then the teachers of reading will have to plan and provide opportunities for their pupils to learn how to demonstrate:

- that they are aware of the complexity;
- that they are thinking about what they are doing;
- that they are able to make meaning in a number of ways.

Pupils not sure how to read focus on decoding and managing individual words, or small bursts of words. The complexity of texts is not something they have been able to recognise, because they are too busy attempting to make the individual words do something. They are mostly unaware of the separate discourses of different sorts of text, and need to realise that texts are actually 'about something'. In the past they will often have been excluded from a 'range of meaning-making' activities, because of the frustration they might have experienced for themselves, or the insistence of concentrating on improving decoding skills adopted by their teachers or other supporting adults. One of the important new approaches enshrined in the National Literacy Strategy is the expectation of all pupils experiencing a balanced reading programme of 'text level', 'sentence level' and 'word level' work (based on the reading knowledges outlined in Chapter 2). In the past, poor readers have usually been locked into 'word level' activities – mostly designed to improve their phonemic awareness. Unfortunately, too much emphasis on that limited area of reading knowledge precludes much study of a range of textual material. Many struggling readers simply forgot that texts are concerned with broader issues than merely beginning the reading process. If you have never considered texts from that perspective, you have no way of knowing that it could be a helpful reading starting point!

Teachers have to help pupils at the earliest stages of secondary education realise that they can be part of wider reading endeavour. Nobody is excluded and the entitlement to reading growth and development applies to every pupil. Even those who do not decode easily can be helped to develop the sorts of reading behaviours more likely to enhance effective reading. To enable all pupils to feel part of this process it is necessary to return to some fundamental starting points for everyone in Year 7, or whatever school year the pupil joins the school. This repositioning should not disadvantage the very capable and more able readers in the class; indeed, properly organised and fully implemented, they should gain considerably from being encouraged to articulate more profoundly what they recognise about their own reading growth. This means of reiterating the starting points of reading will also benefit EAL pupils (those whose first language is not English) who often need to be helped to establish a clearer starting position in a welter of linguistic activities to which they are subjected.

Teaching reading through close language study

George Keith's powerful chapter 'Noticing Grammar' (in the QCA English team document 'Not whether, but how...' 1999), suggests a way of helping pupils pay close attention to the language – and particularly the grammar – of texts they are studying; it is also an effective way of helping pupils realise that texts are very carefully constructed to convey precise meanings. For many less confident or still beginning readers in the secondary school, this method of 'problematising' every word, sentence and paragraph, searching for the ways in which they have coherence within a whole textual context, is a most effective way of teaching reading. Teachers have good reasons to be sceptical of this approach. These pupils, they might well argue, have enough difficulty in decoding the words of the text in the first place. It is surely too much to expect them to be bothering about all sorts of other matters the text might raise.

It is this limited view of reading that has constrained many young people from making the level of progress of which they are capable. A considerable number of poor readers, a large proportion of whom are boys, have given up struggling with texts precisely because they have often attempted to draw meanings out of texts they have real difficulties wading through. All their energies and attention have been devoted to getting to the end of the sentences, or paragraphs, or to the conclusion itself, usually without noticing much of the actual words themselves. The 'extension of phonics' model of teaching reading – with its attendant undemanding worksheets – still evident in some special needs departments, only confirms the pupils in their attitudes about reading being little more than a mechanistic activity, with the expectation of a low level of interpretation. It is also not unusual to see routine, undemanding reading lessons for average and more able readers, in which large swathes of text are read and occasional references are made by teachers to issues of character or plot development, merely to ensure that everyone in the class can comprehend what is taking place. In these circumstances there is no active involvement promoted in the ways the text is working, or the devices and techniques being employed by the author.

I recommend to teachers the notion that every reader ought to be capable of reading any text; the teacher merely has to decide on, and provide, the degree of support necessary to make the engagement worthwhile. No text is out of bounds. In these circumstances, teachers will be interested in devising simple tasks to undertake with complicated texts, to ensure those texts begin to yield increasing meaning. This attitude in school is far more likely to encourage reluctant readers back to committed reading than providing unchallenging and undemanding materials, because they are assumed to be more suitable.

Teachers quite often look back with their classes at the earliest chapters of a book being read – after reading on some way into it, or sometimes having completed it – to help them gain a sense of how the text has developed. My suggestion is that this close study begins from the outset. It is designed as a means of engaging from the start. There are real advantages in setting up all sorts of 'problems' about the text from the outset, establishing a few strands that readers can continue to pursue. Differentiation in reading is possible where teachers are able to urge pupils to follow through different numbers of these strands, depending on their attainment.

I have often sat in library-based, silent reading lessons where boys have mooched along by the bookshelves, selecting a superficially interesting looking text. They have then sat down, opened up the text and attempted to engage with it, but given up after a few lines, or at best a page or two. Many of these boys had insufficient knowledge to allow them to access the text in any significant way. They could read the words, but were unable to attach the meanings of what they were reading in such a way as to provide them with a properly developed catechism to 'interrogate' the text successfully. Many boys enjoy 'doing jobs' with texts; undertaking clearly defined tasks to discover the readily apparent features, which, in turn, makes them more comfortable about speculating on insights into the text using the evidence they have 'discovered'. But they need to be prepared for and rehearse these tasks in systematic ways before attempting them of their own volition. It is as if they require a repertoire of possible questions to put to the text at the very earliest opportunity, otherwise their interest in continuing with the text will simply not be sustained. Not only less confident boys would benefit from this preparation; all readers would more confidently be able to articulate their strategies for making stronger engagements with formerly unknown texts through practising the methods set out in this section.

After having applied this minute study to the early passages of a text it would certainly be helpful to reread the studied section to allow pupils to put their new knowledge of it to work. This approach should then allow pupils to make their way through the rest of the text with many 'strands' of interpretation already active. The readers should not have to wait until the end of the text to draw, retrospectively, on what they have already encountered, but can play a more enactive role with the text as they proceed through it.

Only sections of the text would be subjected to this degree of study in a longer text, such as a novel. Progress would be far too slow otherwise. The beginnings of any text, however, should always be an essential 'engagement point'. This closer engagement with texts would not necessarily have to be a whole–class activity. It could be undertaken with smaller groups of pupils, each group sharing a separate and different text distinct from their classmates. Certainly, it would probably be most helpful to begin from a whole class position, to practise getting closer to the language issues Keith has identified, but greater pupil autonomy would be brought about by moving to more independent study. The 'guided reading' section of Literacy Hour lessons currently being developed in primary classrooms would be an excellent example of introducing this methodology in secondary schools.

Those teachers not convinced about the suitability of this approach to reading for all their readers should look again at the sorts of demands being made on pupils by their most visionary colleagues in the primary school through the National Literacy Strategy. There is considerable evidence that Key Stage 1 and 2 pupils are making improved and more knowledgeable commentaries of their own reading in classrooms where the teaching of reading, through shared and guided reading activities, is being capably planned and implemented. Some of these teachers are beginning to use the techniques of close language study, suitable for their pupils, as outlined in the following paragraphs.

Keith takes as his text *The Sheep Pig* by Dick King-Smith, and he models a way of close analytical study of the first chapter. The pupils are expected to recognise as significant everything they encounter; nothing should be overlooked or taken for granted. Even the chapter headings, where they exist, have some meaning to contribute:

This chapter has a title *Guess my weight.* Notice that it begins with an *imperative verb* (a command) and that the possessive pronoun 'my' implies a personal voice, confirmed by the speech marks. Some readers may hear the echo of another text and context – fairground language – but others may not pick up the reference. Quite apart from the text grammar here, the intriguing title deserves *routine discussion.*

The story begins with *direct speech* by Mrs Hogget. She starts with a question and continues with a series of run-on utterances, a feature of everyday speech that conveys an element of her character. She does in fact use all four sentence functions in her speech which, in sequence, are: question, command, statement (sometimes called declarative), question, exclamation, statement, exclamation, question, command, question (tagged on to the end).

I have been developing a similar programme of textual study for Year 7 and 8 classrooms, deploying, mostly, the opening sections of texts from a range of genres. This device of photocopying the first few paragraphs of five or six different novels for analysis can sometimes serve as a helpful way of introducing texts to a class, then asking the pupils which texts they would prefer to continue reading. There is no doubt that they will be able to offer far more developed arguments to justify their choices as a result of successful engagements undertaken in this manner.

My suggested texts for intense study are the opening or early passages of three novels: Terry Pratchett's *Truckers* (1989); *Eva* by Peter Dickinson (1988); and *Maphead* by Lesley Howarth (1994). These are suitable for all readers in Years 7 or 8 of secondary school, to study in detail, 'noticing grammar' as George Keith suggests.

Truckers – *Terry Pratchett*

No reader will fail to notice that most of the writing on the opening page of *Truckers* is contained within a box (see Example 1). As the page is now split into two parts, it is worth stopping for a moment to consider the whole page, not to begin reading at the beginning. Contained within the box, but slightly apart at the bottom, is a line which reads: '*From* The Book of Nome, *Basements v.I-XII*'. The teacher will probably want to pause to allow pupils to suggest to what previous knowledge this line is alluding. A clue could be afforded by reference to: 'In the beginning...', the only line outside the box. This language should have resonances for a few readers (possibly a diminishing number, which might be another issue to pursue!). The Biblical reference could possibly require some overt comparison with the original. What does the ellipsis following this phrase suggest; why is this device employed? The first mark we encounter in the box is a Roman numeral. Which sorts of texts are set out in numbered fashion? The class will be expected to think of a range of texts, not necessarily fictional narratives. 'There was the Site.' is an intriguing statement, with a puzzling extra capital letter at a point in the sentence where we do not

In the beginning...

I. *There was the Site.*

II. *And Arnold Bros (est. 1905) Moved upon the face of the Site, and Saw that it had Potential.*

III. *For it was In the High Street.*

IV. *Yea, it was also Handy for the Buses.*

V. *And Arnold Bros (est. 1905) said, Let there be a Store, And Let it be a Store such as the World has not Seen hitherto;*

VI. *Let the length of it be from Palmer Street even unto the Fish Market, and the Width of It, from the High Street right back to Disraeli Road;*

VII. *Let it be High even Unto Five Storeys plus Basement! And bright with Lifts; let there be the Eter-nal Fires of the Boiler-Room in the sub-basement and, above all other floors, let there be Customer Accounts to Order All Things;*

VIII. *For this must be what all shall Know of Arnold Bros (est. 1905):* All Things Under One Roof. *And it shall be called: the Store of Arnold Bros (est. 1905)*

ix. *And Thus it Was.*

x. *And Arnold Bros (est. 1905) divided the Store into Departments, of Ironmongery, Corsetry, Modes and others After their Kind, and Created Humans to fill them with All Things saying, Yea, All Things Are Here. And Arnold Bros (est. 1905) said, Let there be Lorries, and Let their Colours be Red and Gold, and Let them Go Forth so that All May Know Arnold Bros (est. 1905), By Appointment, delivers All* Things;

xi. *Let there be Santa's Grottoes and Winter Sales and Summer Bargains and Back to School Week and All Commodities in their Season;*

xii. *And into the Store came the Nomes, that it would be their Place, for Ever and Ever.*

From The Book of Nome, *Basements v.I–XII*

usually encounter them. The author and the editor of this text are experienced language users, so we can reasonably assume that this mark is not a mistake. Once again, the class would ask, where might readers encounter this usage? The next sentence is – as are all subsequent sentences on this page – prefaced by another Roman number. What do we call such 'sentences' in the Bible, and how might this term relate to the 'v' in the sentence at the bottom of the page? This sentence also begins with one of the allegedly 'high crimes' of English grammar; starting a sentence with 'and'! Readers should have plenty to consider regarding this matter, and will want to reflect on all they have been taught about that word. They will move on to discuss who 'Arnold Bros' might be; what function the parentheses and full stop are performing in '(est. 1905)'. Further interest should be engendered through puzzling about the liberal and unusual use of capital letters at the start of 'Moved', 'Saw' and 'Potential'.

The whole of the sentence 'And Arnold Bros (est. 1905) moved upon the face of the Site, and saw that it had Potential.' suggests an anachronistic vocabulary, not normally used in contemporary writing. 'moved upon the face' is unusual, and sustains the references to the King James version of the Bible. Pupils are also likely to suggest that one of the features of texts from earlier centuries is the random manner in which some words begin with capital letters (although readers might look closely to establish whether capital letters are being applied with any rationale). Readers now have a clearer sense of the anachronistic nature of the text in the line prefaced with a 'III': 'For it was In the High Street.' It is also at about this point that they will realise it is safe to smile at what they are reading. Why is this particular combination of words funny? The next line is even better: 'Yea, it was also Handy for the Buses.'

The dawning realisation that the text is designed to have a particular effect on the reader is crucial. Teachers will help pupils prepare for more language of this sort, because the likelihood is that they have realised they are now encountering a humorous text; the clues about the particular genre are quite clear.

'Verse' VII is much longer than any of the previous sentences, comprising about 40 words. Pupils should be alerted early in their reading studies to considering relative sentence lengths, and then be ready to ask themselves what the writer is intending to add to the text by their choices. This is a long sentence, when compared with most other sentences in young people's books, but not when set alongside sentences from the Bible. It is also a crucial sentence in the unfolding of the novel's story, and its contents require close study to ensure that all readers have understood its descriptive implications, in addition to its linguistic interests. (That it resembles the medieval model of the universe is a feature teachers may or may not wish to pursue!) The end of this sentence has much in common with the endings of others in this text: 'Customer Accounts to Order All Things', is similar in its structuring to 'it had Potential', and 'delivers All Things'.

I shall not continue in this detailed manner, but it should be evident that pupils would be offered enormous opportunities of worthwhile interaction, not only whetting their reading appetites, improving the nature of their reading engagements but also considerably enhancing their language knowledge. Just as important, however, is the part being played by this page in awakening the reader's awareness of what the whole text is about. These Biblical allusions are not chance references; they should suggest obvious religious themes likely to occur in the rest of the novel. Further references to *The Book of the Nome*, indeed, are scattered through the text. So, it will be no surprise to alert readers that one of the purposes of the book is to offer a witty and good-natured satire on religious dogma, among other topics. While the superficial reader will think it merely an adventure story featuring a group of Nomes!

Eva *by Peter Dickinson (1988)*

This book is divided into 'Parts', and so before the first page proper of the story there is a virtually blank page, on which part way down is printed 'Part One', and on the next line 'Waking'. Discussion about 'parts' as divisions of books, and pupils' familiarity with them, and the sorts of suggestions triggered by 'Waking', would be a helpful introduction to the study of this text.

The first page begins with a large, capitalised title: 'DAY ONE' (see Example 2). Most pupils will have little difficulty recognising the journal/diary, chronological reference. Quickly scanning through the rest of the text would confirm that that the book is not only divided into parts, but each section – or chapter – within the parts is headed by a time reference.

Then, unusually, the text proceeds not with a paragraph of continuous prose, but a list of italicised words, each followed by ellipsis. The words have a loose relationship:

Waking . . .
Strange . . .
Dream about trees? Oh, come back! Come . . .
Lost . . .
But so strange . . .

These words and phrases all have an insubstantial quality, suggestive of the 'Waking' which opens this part of the book. They also shift us quickly inside a character, experiencing the realisation of the world from a person's point of view. They have further power, in suggesting something that is missing or has gone, and is now not familiar for the character whose awakening consciousness we are being invited to share. The 'trailing away' of the ellipsis would be a worthwhile area of study by the pupils.

But we do not continue pursuing the narrative from the point of view of the character we originally encountered. We are now switched to a new observer's position, through the deployment of the third person voice: 'Eva was lying on her

DAY ONE

Waking...
Strange...
Dream about trees? Oh, come back! Come...
Lost...
But so strange...

Eva was lying on her back. That was strange enough. She always slept face down. Now she only knew that she wasn't by the sensation of upness and downness – she couldn't actually feel the pressure of the mattress against her back. She couldn't feel anything. She couldn't be floating? Still dreaming?

When she tried to feel with a hand if the mattress was there it wouldn't move. Nothing moved! Stuck!

In panic she forced her eyes open. It seemed a huge effort. Slowly the lids rose.

Dim white blur. A misty hovering shape, pale at the centre, dark at the edges.

'Darling?'

With a flood of relief Eva dragged herself out of the nightmare. Mum's voice. The mist unblurred a little, and the shape was Mum's face. She could see the blue eyes and the mouth now.

She tried to smile but her lips wouldn't move.

'It's all right, darling. You're going to be all right.'

There was something terrible in the voice.

'Do you know me, darling? Can you understand what I'm saying? Close your eyes and open them, again.'

The lids moved slow as syrup. When she opened them she could see better, Mum's face almost clear, but still just blur beyond.

'Oh, darling!'

Relief and joy in the voice now, but something else still, underneath.

Example 2: The opening of *Eva* by Peter Dickinson, published by Victor Gollancz 1988. Reproduced by permission of A.P. Watt Ltd on behalf of the author.

back.' Once again, it is helpful to suggest that the pupils think of the relative length of sentences. Most sentences in this paragraph are of this length: five or six words. Only one sentence – the middle one – is much longer, and draws enormous attention to itself by that comparison. 'Now she only knew that she wasn't by the sensation of upness and downess – she couldn't actually feel the pressure of the mattress against her back.' The readers are being taken further and further from a real, concrete situation and encouraged to feel closely, with Eva, that all experience is ethereal. What is this awakening from? Why is it so unusual? How is the language, both the actual words employed and the devices being constructed with them, contributing to the overall meaning of this passage?

'When she tried to feel with a hand if the mattress was there it wouldn't move. Nothing moved! Stuck!' That is the second paragraph. The writer is adding extra layers to the impressions being established through the opening. The short, panic-driven sentences involve the reader in Eva's horror very quickly and forcefully. Notice how the author uses colloquial language, 'wouldn't', rather than the more formal 'would not', to increase the pace of the line. Readers will want to comment on the use of a one word sentence, 'Stuck!', and reflect on its potency in this context. Which part of speech is 'stuck' in this context? What do readers have to add to the word to enable it to make complete sense? Does the language, at this stage, begin to suggest the type of genre(s) in which this text could be categorised, or do readers need a little more acquaintance with the text before such hypotheses can be confirmed?

Other words suggestive of indistinctness, 'blur', 'dim', 'unblurred', 'misty', 'pale at the centre, dark at the edges' are to be found in the next few lines. There are also further references to the constrictive imagery already introduced: 'She tried to smile but her lips wouldn't move', as we learn from Eva's mother that the girl is slowly recovering from a paralysis. Little by little we are being made aware of Eva's condition through the same stages as our central character, and our response to her predicament closely mirrors her own. The early stages of the book will continue in this slow realisation of the hideous condition Eva finds herself in, and our sympathies stay bonded to her appalling struggle for the rest of the book. This underrated novel is a truly frightening and challenging story, very worthy of study in Key Stage 3 classrooms and, despite its female protagonist, of equal interest to boys and girls, if they can be engaged at the very beginning.

Maphead *by Lesley Howarth*

It is almost impossible not to engage the interest of any youthful reader in the first few paragraphs of this novel. The title at the top of the first page is itself bizarrely intriguing: 'CATSHAKE' (see Example 3). What does this word suggest in the reader's mind? All adolescent readers will immediately make an association with 'milkshake' or 'chocolate shake'. What is the activity or thing being referred to here? What could a 'catshake' possibly be?

CATSHAKE

The reason Powers'd liquefied the cat in the end greenhouse first is it asked for it. It was a scrawny grey number with pleating yellow eyes and sticking-out hip bones, like it'd swallowed a box or something. It came mewling around at the slightest niff of food. It'd even beg for tomatoes when it knew it couldn't eat them.

One evening, after a film, Powers turned his eyes on the scrawny grey cat. It was bad news for the cat. Under the power of Powers' eyes it quailed and fell down. It must've heaved in its skin a full ten seconds before its organs reduced. Then there was draining and disposal. And about two pints of catshake. "Enjoy," said Powers. Boothe grinned. He'd only been Boothe ten minutes. Really his name was Map-Head. But already he felt the new name bite.

The end greenhouse was home, for the while. It was the largest of five great glasshouses on the tomato farm – and the furthest from the bungalow. Evenings, they usually wandered up the track and sat in their hollow place in the hedge. It was the ideal angle to catch the telly in the bungalow living-room. They always felt like munchies when they got back. It was just the cat's bad luck.

Example 3. Extract from *MAPHEAD* © 1994 Lesley Howarth
Reproduced by permission of the publisher Walker Books Ltd, London.

The next few lines are unambiguous: 'The reason Powers'd liquefied the cat in the end greenhouse first is it asked for it. It was a scrawny grey number with pleading yellow eyes and sticking-out hip bones, like it'd swallowed a box or something. It came mewling around at the slightest niff of food. It'd even beg for tomatoes when it knew it couldn't eat them.' This paragraph presents a number of language puzzles for the reader. Who is speaking or narrating this text? It is not the usual tone of the third person, detached narrator. It has a point of view on the events taking place in a more direct manner. There are sufficient resemblances to speech ('Powers'd', 'it'd', 'scrawny grey number') to suggest it is almost a first person conversational style. There is also something stilted about the sentence construction of this paragraph, unlike normal English, to hint that language and language style might be central concerns in the telling of this story. The first sentence is extremely direct, but also enigmatic. How does somebody 'liquefy' a cat? What sort of monstrous sensibility is at work here? Where is the moral dimension in the description of this act?

Language continues to be slightly off-centre in the following paragraph. The cat 'quailed', 'heaved' and 'reduced', under the 'power of Powers' eyes' in a way the reader is expected to accept as normal. Two sentences demand attention: 'Then there was draining and disposal. And about two pints of catshake.' It would be more usual in English to write of 'the draining' and 'the disposal', but the author omits the definite article in both instances. The second sentence begins with 'and', again suggesting a much less formal narrator than often employed in novels.

The names of the characters also attract our interest. Are 'Powers' and 'Boothe' first names or surnames? Isn't there a Hollywood actor named Powers Boothe? How could 'Boothe' only have been called that name for 'ten minutes'? What sort of name is 'Map-Head', and what sort of creature does that suggest? And why would this new name 'bite'? Nouns and verbs are apparently playing all sorts of tricks in this early part of the text, establishing all sorts of enigmas for the aware reader.

The next paragraph continues this uneasy manner of storytelling. 'The end greenhouse was home, for the while.' This sentence assumes that we know of the greenhouse, and where it was situated. We are expected to fill in considerable gaps already opening up between what the author reveals and what the reader can be sure of knowing. 'They always felt like munchies when they got back. It was just the cat's bad luck.' We are privy to the colloquial, private language of these two characters, and are gradually being drawn into their way of seeing events. The missing possible exclamation mark at the end of the last sentence suggests a very matter-of-fact attitude to a grotesque event. We are also becoming accustomed to accepting a most unusual set of circumstances, not usual in our world. With a slight shift from the commonplace, the author has manoeuvred her readers into a fantasy which overlaps with the real world.

Keith is not exclusively concerned with narrative fiction in his chapter (QCA 1999) – he also illustrates how it is equally possible to look closely at a non-narrative text. He selects a pamphlet from the NSPCC to analyse, as yet a further model for scrupulous reading.

> The title takes the form of a *question*. The text sets out to answer its own question.

> The first word encountered is 'If', a word that immediately introduces argument. Noticing its rhetorical effect is more helpful practically than knowing it is a *subordinating conjunction* introducing a statement (or clause) that is dependent for its full meaning on another statement (or clause) in the sentence. You could ask, what difference is made by putting the 'if' in the middle of the sentence.

English teachers who begin approaching texts in this way will quickly realise that their own language knowledge has to be brought centre stage, and sometimes supplemented, to ensure that the potential of the text is fully exploited and opportunities are not missed. Some of the language demands of the current Literacy Strategy Framework at Key Stages 1 and 2 have proved challenging to many English teachers in the secondary phase. This has not been wholly surprising, as many of those teachers have not been tutored in language knowledge at any stage of their training, beyond the most superficial.

Wherever possible, teachers should attempt to 'rehearse' this analytical style with colleagues, attempting to anticipate the likeliest suggestions pupils might offer as a result of their scrutinies. One of the interesting and challenging risks this method offers is that pupils may well make suggestions and offer associations of ideas not always forming part of the teacher's own experience.

If English departments adopted this method of carefully reading textual extracts as a way of teaching pupils to read, they would be contributing to a continuing programme to which pupils in primary school are becoming increasingly accustomed. They would also be preparing pupils far more systematically for the rigours of unseen texts likely to be encountered in GCSE examination conditions in Key Stage 4.

Teaching from picture texts

A dramatic way of bringing about more intense attention to textual knowledge by English departments is through the use of picture books. This is far from being an original idea of mine. Reading researchers and those concerned with the broader understanding of text have been suggesting variations of this approach for many years. Some teachers of English might be incredulous that a seemingly superficially trivial resource could be proposed to support and improve the reading of young people aged 11+, especially for those who are already accomplished readers. These books are surely – some might attempt to claim – written for young children and belong in the Key Stage 1 classroom, for early readers. They would be a worthless distraction and waste of time for older readers. I believe that this is a limited and wholly misguided view of a potentially rich vein of valuable materials. Mawdsley (1990) thought similarly:

> Picture books seemed to be conceived more as a rung on the reading ladder – there to support the next inexorable step up, rather than as a complex framework of scaffolding supporting, but also inviting movement in many directions.

> Happily, we now have a heritage of picture books that are read by people of all ages, exploring through skilful illustrations, and sometimes an accompanying text, a range of issues from the personal to the political, from satire to seriousness.

The popularity of illustrated narrative is growing in the United Kingdom, although these texts have often been regarded as no more than 'comics'; a term usually applied derogatorily and meant to show that they are exclusively written for children. In the rest of Europe picture narratives are a respectable way of telling stories for adults: the adventures of Tintin from Belgium and Asterix from France testify to that tradition.

Unless English teachers have small children of their own, they do not have many opportunities to discover much about the enormous variety and potential power of the many picture books currently being published. At a recent INSET course I led, a teacher who had been reading one of these texts with his own child excitedly shared with the other participants his complete conviction that such a book had to be capable of being used with audiences other than the very youngest. He had realised that many of these superficially simple and straightforward texts are actually very deliberately and carefully written, have a number of ways of making complex meanings through the relationship between words and pictures, and are often about enormously important human issues. They are invariably popular with secondary pupils; school librarians who include collections of picture books in their fiction sections always report how dog-eared they become from regular use. Many pupils will remember favourite titles, authors, illustrators and themes from their own earlier reading experiences. Ironically, the group of pupils which most readily rejects them are those who read less confidently. They often regard them as 'kids' books', a perception not helped by a few publishers who sometimes perversely include the legend on back covers such as: 'Suitable for readers aged 5 to 9 years.' The objections of the struggling readers will soon be dispelled when they see these books being given validity by their teachers and more able peers.

One of the most important qualities of picture books (not 'children's picture books' since some of them are no more especially written for children than was Orwell's *Animal Farm!*), making them appropriate for the teaching of reading, is that they can be regarded as an available whole text, possible to be read in only a few minutes, at most. Pupils will not have to struggle through pages of text, over a number of weeks, expected to remember the details of what was read many days previously, before they can engage with the issues it raises. They also help to illustrate the point that reading is the same process for readers wherever they might be placed along a progressive reading continuum.

Yet for all their supposed lightweight nature they are deliberate textual constructs, written to be *about* something, devised in a focused linguistic manner within recognisable genres. They also have an added bonus of the pictures, often working in a wholly symbiotic relationship with the words, to add further clues to meaning in most instances, but, occasionally, adding a witty or enigmatic counterpoint. They have many of the essential characteristics of novels and more developed longer narratives, but they do not have to waded through by – in some instances – reluctant or disenfranchised readers for months before all the parts can be considered together.

During the past two decades there has been an explosion of new picture book titles and the emergence of a huge number of writers and illustrators. Many of these names have become well known to adult audiences too. Some of those writers English teachers might like to read and review for themselves are listed, but this is an arbitrary enterprise and it is not my intention to exclude many suitable and challenging texts. Those who do not know the work of Janet and Allan Ahlberg, Shirley Hughes, Anthony Browne, Brian Wildsmith, Tony Ross, David Macaulay, Chris Van Allsburg, Helen Cooper, Babette Cole, John Burningham, Michael Forman, Jon Scieszka and Lane Smith, Nick Butterworth, Marcus Pfister, Christian Birmingham, Colin Thompson, Quentin Blake, Phillipe Dupasquier, David McKee, Colin McNaughton, Mick Inkpen, Ruth Brown, Martin Waddell and Nick Sharratt could fruitfully begin their research with the texts of these people. Better still, spend a long and happy morning in a good children's bookshop or department, surveying the field for yourself. It will prove to be a most worthwhile investment of time.

Example of a picture book – **Voices in the Park** *by Anthony Browne*

Close scrutiny of Anthony Browne's *Voices in the Park* illustrates how well these texts can be adapted for the secondary classroom, and the major role they are capable of performing in improving pupils' reading. This text is itself a development of a previous book by Browne entitled *A Walk in the Park*, originally published in 1977. The relationship between the two texts would be excellent ground for initial exploration by pupils of all abilities, as everybody would find something to comment about. Less accomplished readers would be able to contribute perceptions on the clear differences, but also the many similarities, between the two versions. Pupils are often placed in better positions to learn about texts if they are able to compare two or more. Reading texts alongside each other makes it possible for less accomplished readers to discover starting points to assert more confident judgements about the reasons why writers/illustrators have made their authorial decisions, and to what purpose.

Briefly, both books share a simple plot of a working class father and daughter, and their dog, visiting a park simultaneously with a middle class mother, her son and their dog. The parents make no contact, but the children and the dogs establish relationships through shared play, cheering them up and improving a not very promising outing. The two books represent clear stages in Anthony Browne's authorial career. *A Walk in the Park* was written and drawn at a time when Browne wrote simple and straightforward, witty and amusing narratives, which gained considerably in their humour from his startling surreal illustrations. An excellent example of his characteristic work of that period can be seen in *Bear Hunt* (1979), where the fun of the written text is enhanced by the riot of unrelated images scattered through the pictures. *A Walk in the Park* is similarly illustrated. The front cover alone is typical; park gates have one side supported by a brick wall, the other a decorated pillar. The left hand portal is decorated with a bowler hat, the right hand side by a small red ball. Incongruous and unusual ideas, such as pigs on leads and hippos in fountains, are to be found on every page. *Voices in the Park* does not wholly dispense with these visual tricks, but they are more discretely and sparingly used, often casting further pointed comment on the characters.

Every teacher would be interested in discovering from their class the possible reasons why Browne has changed the title from *A Walk in the Park* to *Voices in the Park*. Whereas the *Walk* begins to explore the idea of contrasting characters, *Voices* makes more explicit statements about the people who feature in the story. To make this characterisation much clearer, Browne employs four different fonts, each one representing a separate person. So, the 'controlling' middle class mother tells her version of the events in a confident, formal typeface. The unhappy working class father tells his story in a bold, undecorated font. The woman's son, relating the third narrative, is written in a manner imitating his mother, but in a thinner, weaker way. The girl's version is told in a typeface resembling lively handwriting.

But Browne goes yet a stage further. We are not only informed about the differences between these characters from the way their stories look on the page, but we are also helped to see into their separate personalities by the language that each employs. The woman writes in very precise Standard English: 'It was time to take Victoria, our pedigree Labrador, and Charles, our son, for a walk.' The nouns in apposition (a phrase worth sharing with the pupils in this context), the actual names of son and dog, and the structuring of this sentence all contribute to the insights we can make about this mother. 'It was time...', placed at the beginning of her narrative, indicates something of her timetabled existence. It is as important as her reference to the 'scruffy mongrel' euphemistically 'bothering' her own dog a page later. She 'orders' her son to sit near her, continues to 'plan' other happenings while in the park and disapproves of her son's association with the other child, described as 'very rough-looking'. The father approaches the walk in a wholly different way, and has unrelated motives: 'I needed to get out of the house, so me and Smudge took the dog to the park.' His narrative – not in standard English – is sad and depressed, but punctuated with words of hope, mostly supplied through the support of his daughter. The little boy uses many words suggesting the captivity of his life, while his new companion is more down to earth and full of vigour in the vocabulary she is ascribed. His comments are wistful: 'I wished I was', 'Mummy caught us talking'; while hers are more energetic: 'We both burst out laughing', 'I felt really, really, happy.'

There is one more stage of meaning-making in which all pupils can engage to confirm some of the judgements they should now be capable of making about these characters. The pictures leave the reader in few doubts about Browne's intentions. The park the mother sees is, in Browne's own words (1999):

> Very ordered and tidy (the only litter we see is trapped in the cage-like litter-bin), the trees have been trimmed into comfortably plump shapes, and everywhere we see reassuringly rich autumnal colours. She's annoyed at her son's behaviour so I tried to show her smouldering resentment and burning anger in the tree that seems to have caught fire.

While with his mother in the park, the son is usually depicted as literally 'in her shadow', until he escapes to play with Smudge. The other characters are also given their own contexts, represented by seasons of the year, and pupils will have no trouble recognising why, but they will find plenty of opportunity to amplify their findings, to support their increasing knowledge of those featured in the text.

This text is a rich resource for teaching reading. From it, young people should be able to learn to extrapolate information from fiction texts, recognising that writers make their meanings on a number of levels in complementary ways; through the plot, the setting, the characterisation and – not always regarded closely enough – the language. Even those pupils regarded as 'poor' or even, in some instances, 'non' readers will be empowered to take part in critical studies of a sophisticated nature. While the more accomplished readers will make many obvious connections from this study, they should then be urged, through proper opportunities, to express their findings in more developed ways.

A teacher intending to use this text, subscribing to the Qualities and Principles outlined in Chapter 4, would then shape the planning of *Voices in the Park* deliberately to bring about pupils' improved learning in the awareness that:

1. A reader knows that reading is a complex, intellectual endeavour, requiring a range of active meaning-making skills.

If the teacher is comparing *A Walk in the Park* with *Voices in the Park* as part of the learning process, this exercise would help learning in that:

2. A reader draws on previous knowledge of other texts to enable the effective reading and further meaning-making of the text being read.

To meet the needs of the more able readers, the same textual material could also be used as the basis for learning that:

3. A reader is aware that one way of demonstrating progression in reading can be through raising more complex questions about the same text.

The challenge for teachers and pupils will be to gain increasing confidence in raising a more focused variety of questions in relations to texts.

It would be unlikely that anybody would ostensibly want to improve learning of more than two or three principles at once; it is also more helpful for pupils to be able to concentrate on clear, uncluttered learning objectives. If pupils are to be asked to review their own learning, they should only be asked to comment on the improvement they have made in a selected area.

Having made it possible for less confident readers to find greater success in their attempts to delve more closely inside texts, teachers might try to sustain the involvement of those pupils by not necessarily insisting that pupils always record their findings in written forms. It is possible to make an assessment of how well pupils have fulfilled these tasks without the pupils always having to provide written responses. If writing is thought to be desirable or necessary, however, teachers should explore ways of 'scaffolding' their responses, so that pupils are able to demonstrate what they have discovered, without being unnecessarily penalised by a process they do not naturally master.

Other picture texts to teach reading

John Burningham has written many picture books for children, and he is a favourite with small children for stories such as *Mr Gumpy's Outing* and *Mr Gumpy's Motor Car*. Young beginner readers enjoy *Granpa*, but not many return to it without prompting, as its meanings are not immediately evident to those who have little familiarity with texts. The book, quite simply, is about some moments, through the space of a year, in the relationship between a little girl and her grandfather. They chatter away to each other, but not in connected dialogue; in fact, they only speak a line each on every double page, but we are invited imaginatively to fill the missing pieces of talk, to provide the real meaning.

Watson (1996), writing of a study he conducted using this text in a Cambridge-shire infants' school, states:

Granpa is about an old man's past as well as a little girl's present. She is part of a continuity which reveals itself in fragments and opens out *backwards*, ultimately in the final picture suggesting that the past and the future are capable of some kind of magical or conceptual convergence. Granpa is innocent of didactic intentions but he nevertheless passes on to the little girl seminal cultural scraps which become part of her complex and often ambiguous learning. She learns about playing in summer back gardens, about the past, about the strange cultural practices associated with 'a day at the seaside', about sexual embarrassment, and that adults can be hurt. And she learns about love. She presumably makes her own structure of these fragments but, since readers are told nothing of either the process or the product, they must do the work themselves.

This text therefore offers a rich potential for study. The least confident readers can be drawn into closer speculation, suggesting meanings, as a way of recognising the very necessary knowledge that texts do not enshrine single, fixed meanings. They are given opportunities to feel more comfortable in the presence of texts through these learning devices, developing sets of questions to enable each text to yield a range of possible meetings. More accomplished readers will, as Watson's commentary indicates, also discover a broad range of study lines of enquiry to follow.

I once offered this text to a mixed ability group of Year 7 pupils, inviting them to read it. They were given fifteen minutes to discover and discuss at least six things they thought the book might be about. After a slow start, because this was not a familiar line of study, they quickly became adept at offering suggestions based firmly on the evidence of the text: relations between generations, how we represent the world, being old, being young, being a grandparent, being a granddaughter, imagination, memory, loss and mourning, the past, the passing of time, were the sorts of responses they came up with. These responses were not made exclusively by the more able readers in the class.

Another title, *Time to get out of the Bath, Shirley*, is like *Granpa* in a few respects, but very unlike it in others. Pupils will easily recognise Burningham's characteristic style of illustration, and be able to talk about that feature. They will also quickly tune into the way that two separate narratives are being conducted, on opposite pages. Shirley is taking a bath. Her mother, fussing about in the bathroom, conducts a monologue haranguing her daughter for her shortcomings. None of this criticism touches Shirley, who is imagining herself in a fantasy world, represented entirely by pictures. It is a world composed of many diverse images, however, themselves redolent of many stories and fantasy characters.

The work of Raymond Briggs deserves very particular mention. Briggs has written and illustrated a wide range of stories and wordless texts during the past thirty years, from the depiction of nuclear holocaust in *When the Wind Blows*, through the philosophic *The Man* (1992), to the intimate biography of his parents, *Ethel and Ernest* (1998). I want to spend a bit of space considering the teaching merits of *Fungus the Bogeyman* (1977) and the powerfully wordless *The Snowman* (1978).

Fungus the Bogeyman is certainly among the most dense of picture texts. It deals with language in a multitude of ways. The story is about a Bogey family, who inhabit the 'wet, dripping tunnels of Bogeydom', an inverted world that mirrors and overlaps our own, but has utterly different expectations of lifestyle! The text is an amazingly witty mix of puns, literary references, spoof reference material, narrative, speech bubbles and invented vocabulary, (e.g. immediately after waking, Fungus visits the 'barathrum', which, we are told, is a 'pit, chasm, abyss of mud'!). Each page is almost too difficult for the eye to cope with, there is so much happening. Every reader will engage with different parts of the text. Any class of Key Stage 3 pupils will require little prompting to become involved in close study, and all ability groups will be challenged and satisfied by the richness of the material. At one level, this is a text possible to analyse as a way of discovering a range of text types; at another level, the references to literary texts – obscure and well known – will absorb even the most accomplished (e.g. a Bogey library containing such titles as: '*Anna of the Five Bogeys*', '*Cider with Bogey*', and '*A Room with a Bogey*'!) The story is straightforward, and will be easily followed by all readers, but it is uncompromising in the sort of language employed. Pupils who read with difficulty, however, will have sufficient motivation to find their way around the less accessible portions of the book.

Wordless texts

Briggs has also published a text, *The Snowman*, in the growing tradition of wordless texts, worthy of close attention in the classroom. Shirley Hughes' *Up and Up* (1979), Quentin Blake's *Clown* (1995) and any of Martin Handford's utterly absorbing *Where's Wally* series are other notable, but by no means exclusive, examples.

Wordless texts present pupils with infinite possibilities of meaning making. They usually contain a very clear narrative, but the *manner* of narration is not established. The first challenge for pupils is to tell part of the story to each other. They might then attempt to tell the same story, but in different ways, reaching for another narrative style, or fashioning their tale for another audience, perhaps younger than themselves. The pictures will both constrain and liberate the storyteller. The narrator has to obey the conventions of the illustrations, it is not possible to suggest a character might be unhappy when it is quite evidently sporting a huge grin. There are, however, any number of possible ways of shaping the details of the story, merely suggested by the images.

Teaching reading through preparing for writing

A lot of secondary pupils dutifully read the texts selected for them in classrooms, and then expect to be asked to write a few pieces of work for their teacher. These might be responses to what has just been read, or they could be about tracing the growth of a character featured in the text. Every so often, they might be asked to write an argument 'Why is school uniform necessary?', or a leaflet persuading visitors to a dolphinarium, for instance. Sometimes, a class will be given the task of composing a narrative fiction, occasionally but not often modelled on a text studied together.

I would like to explore ways in which reading and writing could be more overtly presented to pupils as a 'package'. They can be helped to regard reading and writing as fundamentally related – they are ways of looking at the same textual material from opposite directions. As the National Literacy Framework document (DfEE 1998) points out:

> Both reading and writing use work at word, sentence and text levels. The context of pupils' reading, i.e. the texts, gives structures, themes and purposes for much of their writing, while the focused teaching of word and sentence level skills contributes to the organisation and accuracy of their writing.

My concern throughout this book has been to increase the reading capability of all pupils, of whatever ability, and most of my recommendations can quickly be applied for everybody's benefit. There are, however, many young people who experience enormous difficulties when confronted with some reading and most writing tasks in the early days of their secondary schools. These pupils have to be supported very carefully, and offered tangible structures to restore belief in themselves about their literacy potential. They have to be helped to restore their often battered morale, and be convinced that they can work independently and make progress. This group, particularly, have to be assisted in their recognition of the relationship between reading and writing, but all other pupils would gain real benefit from this approach.

The way of working I am proposing develops naturally from Keith's work, explained in the first part of this chapter. As pupils look closely at the texts they are reading in the classroom, identifying the grammatical and linguistic characteristics of them, so they also attempt to reconstruct similar texts employing the devices they have highlighted. They could be building texts at word level, sentence level, text level, or all three. The texts could be fiction or non-fiction, drawing on the increasing knowledge pupils would be acquiring about text types and genres. The real point is to help them see themselves as authors, capable of constructing purposeful texts, which have the ability to make planned effects on readers in controlled and predetermined ways. As authors they will be explaining why they are making the textual choices they do, and through this articulation there is greater chance of them realising how published authors work.

While some pupils will write with ease in this approach, the majority will require more initial 'scaffolded' help, possibly encouraged to explore some paragraphs or areas of their work unaided. A few young people, really struggling to know where to begin in, for instance, storytelling, description, or argument, might need intensive help to make any real progress. Many teachers are aware of and already use the *Writing Frames*, published as a result of the research of Wray and Lewis (1997) who were seeking ways of helping pupils write more effective non-fiction as a tool for learning. An essential principle in the use of these frames is the 'teacher modelling' at the beginning of the process. This would equate and link with analysis in Keith's noticing language, where the teacher assists the class to discover the ways in which the text is constructed, as the first step in writing their own versions.

Those boys who are sometimes reluctant to venture far into writing experiences, or who are unlikely to experiment to any degree, can be given substantial toe-holds into textual material on which to build attempts of their own. They could be asked to write sentences of specific lengths, in a precise word patterning ('with the verb at the end, to emphasise the fear of the character'). The requirement might be to compose contrasting sentence lengths, each perhaps with a specified number of clauses, punctuated in a particular way. They could be asked to write a paragraph of so many sentences, building to a tension in a rhetorical manner. They could be asked to use related groups of adjectives, as a means of exploring imagery.

All these very clear tasks would be enhanced and within the reach of more pupils if they had been made aware of 'noticing' the ways the texts on which their own writing was being modelled were actually constructed. They have to be attending to the original textual material in such a way that they cannot fail to improve their own reading abilities. The very best writers can be assisted in coming up with excellent and totally convincing pastiches of a range of writers if they are drawn closely into this process. Those pupils who need more support will always have clearly identified structural frameworks on which to build their own attempts, and which will contribute to their textual insights.

Teaching reading to the least able and most reluctant pupils

All of the recommendations made about teaching reading in this chapter are suitable for teaching all pupils. The support required by those pupils, often but not exclusively boys, who find reading difficult or who are not natural readers without much urging, will obviously be greater than for most pupils, but the principles remain the same. Teachers will have to ascertain if there are particular sorts of problems preventing these young people from making progress, such as poor phonemic skills, but these should be remedied within a broad reading programme, comprising text level, sentence level and word level tuition.

Teachers can make better progress with all pupils if they have been able to discover a comprehensive reading biography for each individual. Pupils who are sometimes described as 'non-readers' are, in fact, getting through masses of textual material, but it is not the sort of reading likely to be legitimate in school! The quotation by Terry Reynolds on page 36 reminds us of the enormous extent of boys' reading, beyond school. Boys are often experts about certain sorts of text. My 14-year-old son will not read much fiction, except in the form of 'Warhammer' games material. These are complex fantasy tales, drawing on sub-Tolkien-like, violent goings-on among heavily weaponed gangs. The rules for each game are massively complicated, yet he and his friends sail through them, constantly cross-referencing and disputing matters of detail.

Boys, like all readers, have to see a point to reading, particularly reading in the ways of the English classroom. They have to be clear about what they are expected to do and the nature of the responses they are supposed to make. Many, although not all, are unlikely to make personal responses unless they have been able to work out what is going on in the text from a different viewpoint. The close study described in the early part of this chapter is always a helpful first step to allow reluctant boys a way into the text. Once they have established what is happening, and they can explain some of the features of what is happening, they can then be helped to move to the next stage. What does the author want us to see as the purpose the writing? The actual language of the text becomes as important as the emotional response, in fact even those pupils more prepared to react with their feelings gain better insights from knowing this study approach.

It is essential to know the details of a pupil's literacy biography if the school hopes to re-engage reluctant readers, boys and girls. This is partly necessary to counteract some myths connected with pupils' reading habits, e.g some reluctant readers do not read at all, boys prefer non-fiction texts. Neither of these statements is a reliable guide – some young people who do not read naturally in school read in other settings, many boys take part in reading of fiction, but not the sort endorsed by the school. It is also necessary to know what might inhibit readers; any personal difficulties about reading; possible obstructive attitudes to reading from home and friends; misconceptions about reading not detected and dealt with at an earlier stage. Teachers reporting on a successful strategy to raise reading achievement of boys in Lewisham (Bisiker and Pidgeon 1998) state:

> We use the Secondary Language Record in Year 7. Pupils have an individual reading conference to talk about their reading histories and reading preferences. Again this helps us to get a good picture of individuals as readers. Pupils have self assessment sheets which help to monitor their own reading development. This system is run in conjunction with the library and within the wider climate of publicising reading across the school and making sure it extends well beyond 'English'.

Reacting positively to their pupils' interests, and purchasing books selected by the pupils for the book boxes supporting reading, has caused many boys to regain an enthusiasm for reading.

Because the first texts that most pupils encounter in their earliest reading stages are invariably fiction, it is important that the sorts of experience captured in those books echoes real or imaginative possibilities of the readers. We have plenty of evidence that many boys do not read fiction beyond the age of eight or nine years, and part of the reasons for this decline might be explained by their inability to relate the books to their own experiences, at a number of levels. Firstly, the subject matter of the book has to touch a point of known or sought awareness in the reader. Secondly, if as the eminent teacher James Britton claimed, 'we read ourselves', the text has to mirror the reader in some respect and confirm the reader's perceptions sufficiently to encourage enough effort to discover more within it. A vital area of our own identity, and one beginning to grow in prominence in the self-perception of junior school children is that of gender. To develop in reading, readers need to 'hear' the text come alive in their own heads, almost to 'live' the text. If, through their own culturally-based, gendered sense of themselves, boys are unable to relate to the experiences they are encountering on the page, they will be less willing to return for further encounters. Barrs and Pidgeon (1998) explore this relationship in more detail in their study of *Boys and Reading*, where they state:

> Although at a particular point in their development they may seem intent on classifying the world into exaggeratedly male and female sectors and aligning themselves with exaggerated versions of masculinity and femininity, we know that with more experience from reading these early concepts are likely to be complicated in a helpful way as they begin to perceive a wider range of possible ways of being.

The 'more experience' has to be supplied by teachers working with clear objectives and well-chosen methodologies, challenging and supporting growing readers at a delicate stage.

Similarly, to encourage pupils from other cultures, where the first language of the home is not English, requires teachers to discover what literacy knowledge those young people might have from their own background. It is not possible to expect pupils to make enormous leaps across chasms of meaning without offering some 'bridging' supports. They must be able to refer, for instance, to themes, ways of telling stories, how texts are woven in patterns that already strike chords, before the gap-filling required by so many textual interactions become a worthwhile pursuit.

Ultimately, however, teachers have to reconsider some of the agenda about reading raised in the early chapters of this book, to ask how an approach to reading, particularly 'schooly' English reading, could be generated which suits more readers in a more rewarding search for meaning. Millard (1997) claims:

...a large proportion of teenage fiction chosen for sharing in the classroom is written in the first person, from the point of view of the main character, dealing in relationships and the development of character, rather than on delineation of the physical world through an omniscient narrator. Teachers invite their pupils to become spectators of other people's lives and draw them into speculation concerning motivation and plausibility of their actions. This mode of reading is more frequently associated with women's reading rather than men's, and is reflected in women's choice of popular genres of fiction (romance, family sagas) but also of magazines and television programmes (soaps, dramas).

There are many different ways of reading. English departments have become accustomed to a very limited range of searching through texts, for a restricted set of reasons. The way we involve those who are proving the most difficult to convince about reading (mostly boys) in a rapidly changing society – where the reading demands are also changing – cannot be delayed for too long. Broadening the possible approaches to texts is one important way of inviting pupils to engage with them.

Children's and picture books discussed in this chapter

Blake, Quentin (1995) *Clown*. Jonathan Cape.
Briggs, Raymond (1998) *Ethel and Ernest*. Jonathan Cape.
Briggs, Raymond (1997) *The Snowman*. Hamish Hamilton.
Briggs, Raymond (1982) *When the Wind Blows*. Hamish Hamilton.
Briggs, Raymond (1997) *Fungus the Bogeyman*. Hamish Hamilton.
Briggs, Raymond (1992) *The Man*. Julia Macrae.
Browne, Anthony (1997) *Voices in the Park*. Hamish Hamilton.
Browne, Anthony (1979) *Bear Hunt*. Hamish Hamilton.
Browne, Anthony (1998) *A Walk in the Park*. Doubleday.
Burningham, John (1970) *Mr Gumpy's Outing*. Jonathan Cape.
Burningham, John (1977) *Come Away from the Water, Shirley*. Jonathan Cape.
Burningham, John (1978) *Mr Gumpy's Motor Car*. Jonathan Cape.
Burningham, John (1978) *Time to Get Out of the Bath, Shirley*. Jonathan Cape.
Burningham, John (1984) *Granpa*. Jonathan Cape.
Dickinson, Peter (1988) *Eva*. Victor Gollancz.
Handford, Martin (1987) *Where's Wally*. Walker Books.
Howarth, Lesley (1984) *Maphead*. Walker Books.
Hughes, Shirley (1979) *Up and Up*. The Bodley Head.
King-Smith, Dick (1983) *The Sheep Pig*. Victor Gollancz.
Pratchett, Terry (1989) *Truckers*. Doubleday.

Chapter 6
Teaching Reading in Subjects Other than English

> Whatever the age range of pupils we teach or whatever our subject speciality, we are concerned in some ways with pupils' reading. As pupils proceed through the school, they increasingly read for learning and enrichment of experience. We cannot assume that these reading purposes will automatically be managed by the majority of pupils. Our common concern is, therefore, how we are to go about teaching pupils something about the varieties of writing they will meet without making reading into a sterile exercise. (Littlefair 1991)

Any teacher introducing a text to a class of pupils has to accept the teaching responsibility of ensuring that the text has meaning for all those pupils. Different sorts of texts require different reading approaches and skills. This is not a recent requirement. The Bullock Report (DES 1975) made this recommendation. More recently, the 1995 National Curriculum Statutory Orders in art, design and technology, geography, history, information technology, mathematics, music and science (DFE 1995) have been prefaced with the following paragraph:

> Pupils *should be taught* to express themselves clearly in speech and writing and *to develop their reading skills*. [my emphasis]. They should be taught to use grammatically correct sentences and to spell and punctuate accurately in order to communicate effectively in written English.

Not many teachers have read that part of the document.

There is considerable research evidence (Lunzer and Gardner 1979; Webster *et al.* 1996) to show that reading is not used in most secondary classrooms as an integral learning feature. Schools make little effort to improve the efficient reading of their pupils. Reading is an almost incidental activity in many lesson settings, usually happening in bursts of about fifteen seconds, as background to a further task (e.g. answering questions, following instructions). Lunzer and Gardner, in fact, described 'a retreat from print' in most classrooms they researched, and modern findings suggest that situation has not improved during the intervening twenty years since their work.

Knowledge of text types or non-fiction genres

Pupils in Key Stages 1 and 2 have to become more acquainted with the ways that

- recount,
- procedural,
- non-chronological report,
- persuasive,
- argument,
- discursive

texts work, to enable them to read and write those text types independently with increasing confidence. The National Literacy Strategy (NLS) sets out a clear programme, and primary teachers have been developing their skills in these areas with enormous alacrity. Their secondary counterparts will soon realise that 11-year-old pupils will be arriving in their new schools with considerably more knowledge about different text types than has ever been seen before. The receiving teachers have to be able to continue developing pupils' knowledge from that position.

The text types selected by the writers of the NLS *Framework* document (DfEE 1998), for study in infant and junior schools are not, by any means, the only texts young readers will encounter. They just happen to be the likeliest set of texts they will come across in their schools in the earlier stages of information gathering. Almost all researchers concerned with exploring how pupils' knowledge of non-fiction can be improved have begun with these same five or six categories.

Webster *et al.*, describing and analysing a longitudinal study of literacy engagements in primary and secondary schools, offer a helpful table of literacy genres across the school (see Figure 6.1).

Why is it necessary for pupils and teachers to know about these genres? Why should teachers have to bother about teaching reading? Why is it not possible for pupils to be taught the contents of the subject, in the traditional way, and pick up the techniques as they get used to them?

The first important piece of information all teachers should know is that readers do not read different sorts of texts in the same way (Webster *et al.* 1996).

A proficient reader in some contexts may be relatively unproficient in others. Rather than thinking of the cognitive components of reading as skills or abilities we should see them as processes requiring specific opportunities to become practices, which change when performed in a variety of contexts.

The types of text and the purposes for reading them actually change the nature of the interaction between reader and text. We do not read fiction in the

Type of writing	Characteristics	Curriculum area
Personal account	First person account of direct experience. Writer organises material by time to 'tell about' events. e.g. account of a family holiday	All subjects, particularly English, PSE, CDT
Report	Objective account of an incident or activity. Third person account of what took place, specifying actions of information in a time sequence. e.g. Experiment to find boiling point of different liquids	All subjects, particularly Science or Geography
Imaginative	First person account of an imagined experience involving writer in role of another. Creation of a context, characters and a time sequence. e.g. Letter home from the trenches during First World War	English, History, PSE
Instruction	Instructions which direct reader to a goal. Specification of steps and ordering of information in a chronological sequence. e.g. operating procedure for a video-recorder	Science, CDT, Home Economics, Maths
Explanation	Objective interpretation of events or mechanisms. Causal relationships and technical vocabulary in a sequential chain of events. e.g. Effect of crop failure in Brazil on High Street coffee prices in United Kingdom	Geography, Science, CDT
Description	Selection of information which describes appearance and properties of an object or phenomenon. Third person factual, objective style. e.g. Description of an Iron Age hill fort	Science, Geography, History, CDT, Home Economics, Modern Languages
Opinion	Presenting a personal viewpoint supported by arguments or examples. Selection and organization of subjective information around a theme. e.g. Article on effects of violent videos on young people	All subjects
Narrative	Relating a story with plot, characters and sequence of events to entertain an audience. e.g. Science fiction story	English
Information	Formal, objective writing emphasising factual information, attempts to classify, using technical vocabulary or graphic devices. e.g. Information on pollution of British beaches	All subjects
Persuasion	Attempt to influence reader to a particular course of action or belief. e.g. Advertising leaflet	English, History, PSE, RE
Compare and Contrast	Balanced and objective treatment setting out similarities and differences between two or more topics. e.g. Properties of metals/non-metals	All subjects
Reflection	Personal response to experience, organised thematically. e.g. Views on living through a bereavement	English, RE, PSE
Argument	Development of a logical argument supported by evidence. e.g. Case for legalizing euthanasia	All subjects
Analysis	Impartial and systematic exploration of a problem, evaluating conflicting evidence to draw objective conclusions. e.g. Patterns of poverty and health in different social groups	All subjects

Figure 6.1 Literacy genres across the school curriculum. Reproduced by kind permission of Taylor & Francis/Routledge from Webster, A., Beveridge, M. and Reed, M. (1996) *Managing the Literacy Curriculum.*

same way that we read non-fiction, and even the way we read fiction will depend on factors well beyond the text itself (Traves 1994):

> The meaning made by the reader depends in part on the situation in which the reading takes place. Reading *Jane Eyre* on the beach as part of holiday relaxation is quite different to reading it for a GCSE examination or as part of a PhD on the construction of women in nineteenth-century literature. In all three cases the words on the page remain the same but the experience and meaning of the reading varies significantly.

Lunzer and Gardner (1984) state:

> A growing body of evidence shows that one of the reasons for failure to go beyond local sense is that children often take it for granted that to read correctly is to understand, as if recognising the words and what they mean is all there is to it.

They point out that a gripping story seems to be read in that way; some reading commentators talk of the 'book reading the reader' in those circumstances. Most reading for information and subject-based reading is undertaken quite differently. Much of it requires the reader to skim and scan for potentially useful passages, to make repeated readings and rereadings of passages to establish and check for meaning, to pause reflecting on ideas, and for ongoing summarisation, to enable the reader to 'bind' the information together.

There are few academics, researchers and teachers these days concerned with the study of language growth who do not agree that language acquisition and development are socially based. That is, language is not just there in the ether, to be picked up and honed by each of us in some abstract, detached way. We do not just 'get language', it exists in social contexts, and each of those contexts has its own frameworks and rules for conducting its language interactions. The rules are not absolute and exclusive, they overlap and the edges are sometimes blurred, but there is sufficient differentiation between them to make them worth categorising. The realms of science differ from those of historical study, the language of business and management is unlike that of sports coaching. The practitioners of these different institutions have, through their enthusiasm and commitment, been gradually apprenticed into their ways, and no longer regard the language framing their discourses as problematic. To many pupils, the language of their school subjects presents huge barriers, preventing real engagement. The language, to put it bluntly, can get in the way of the learning. If we learn through language, and prove that learning has taken place by using language, then language is central in the learning process. Pupils' perception of the subjects they study is constructed through language: the teachers' most demanding task is to make that language transparent and accessible for their pupils.

In Chapter 4, a number of qualities of a reader were outlined which are intended to apply to all readers, whatever the context of their reading. Quality number 3 states:

- a reader is aware that texts are constructed for particular purposes, for identifiable audiences and within recognisable text types or genres.

If every teacher in the school is collaborating to enhance the reading abilities of all their pupils then there should be some agreement about the qualities of a reader they would be working together to improve. Littlefair (1991) claims:

> So we are being urged to look at various types of writing in terms of their individual meanings. This seems a very involved task, but if we can differentiate and categorize these types according to the particular meanings they express, we will be in a position to plan our pupils' reading strategically. When authors set out to express their meaning, they have very definite purposes. We will find it very much easier to categorize the meanings of various types of writing if we look for the purposes of the writers.

So it is not unreasonable to encourage and support pupils spending some time in their engagements with texts, seeking the purposes of those texts, and in so doing to also consider how the meanings have been made.

A pupil who knows something about the differences between types of text is likely to be aware that **recounts** begin with an orientation, establishing a central focus for the piece of writing, allowing the reader a starting point relative to other events:

'Last week our class visited the Science Museum.'

'During this term my group has been studying the effects of sunlight on plants.'

'Queen Victoria's reign began in 1837.'

A good recount will supply a timeline for the reader; it could be very short, as in a physics experiment, or very long, relating to geological periods, but the reader should be able to follow the stages. One of the linguistic features of this text type is the use of words and phrases related to time:

'then,' 'next', 'when we had finished', 'later that day', 'during the next stage', 'in 1642'.

Teachers of science and history will quickly realise that they are regularly using recount texts in their classrooms, as the predominant text type of their subject textbooks, and in writing tasks expected of pupils. It should be quite obvious that where teachers refer to this sort of knowledge in their textual interactions with their classes, they will continually reinforce their pupils' awareness of and confidence in this genre. A ready contrast could be made with **explanations** or **explanatory texts**. These are not concerned with *when* events happened, or their sequences over time, but with *how* things work, *why* something is a particular shape, and the reasons for things happening, among others. They usually begin by helping the reader understand the problem being considered: 'how fish swim', 'why the sea is salt', 'why Hitler invaded Czechoslovakia'. Because some explanatory texts consider events or phenomena in sequential order, they sometimes share, with recounts, language related to time: 'first', 'the next stage', 'when that is finished'. Quite unlike recounts, however, is the usage of cause and effect: 'because', 'as a consequence', 'to make... happen', 'if'. They are also usually constructed in the continuous present tense, 'are', 'happens', 'turns into', unlike recounts which can only be written in the past tense as they refer to events already complete. I am not suggesting or recommending that teachers of subjects other than English should spend a large proportion of any lesson specifically teaching the sorts of points I have explained in the previous paragraphs. Indeed, if they have already been introduced into the literacy culture of the school, there would be little need to continue to teach them. A regular update and reminder of these topics could be the most helpful ways of preparing for any textual encounter.

'Can anybody remember what we call this form of text?'

'How did you know it was recount/ explanation/ discursive?'

'Which features of language should we looking out for when reading/writing?'

and just as importantly:

'When you write up your work, will you please remember to include the following features...'

If pupils knew they were also being assessed on their more accurate use of particular text types, they would be prepared to pay considerably closer attention to their own written efforts, and read through their material more thoroughly to check that it satisfied the expected conditions. Pupils would see through this association, yet again, how reading and writing are integrally linked.

Derewianka (1990) calls this sort of preparatory and supporting talk about texts 'A Functional Approach to Language'. All the teachers in a school adopting this 'functional' approach would soon positively transform the literacy and language culture in which more effective learning can take place. Teachers wanting to know more about the linguistic and structural features and details of a wider range of non-fiction genres than I have been able to demonstrate here should refer to Beverly Derewianka's book, or to Lewis and Wray (1995). Although both books were written for an audience of primary teachers, their contents are just as appropriate for secondary teachers, particularly teachers without a great deal of linguistic background.

Directed Activities Related to Texts (DARTS)

It seems extraordinary that only a minority of teachers know much about DARTS. They were contained in Lunzer and Gardner's work (1984), written as a result of the study of reading in schools, following the findings of the Bullock Report. Harrison (1995) states their proposals were:

> ...not so much improvements on comprehension exercises as radical alternatives to them, designed not only to encourage active approaches to reading, but to redefine the relationship between author, reader and text....

All these activities tended to place the reader alongside the author as meaning maker, rather than to position the reader as a passive recipient of knowledge, transmitted from the author. Lunzer's work remains enormously important, in that, some years ahead of its time, it encouraged the notion that texts are an archaeological site for exploring human meaning, rather than a cemetery from which meaning is exhumed.

Unfortunately, they have made little impression on general reading practices in schools in the fifteen years since their publication.

The original DARTS recommendations have been amended since their introduction, as teachers have added more activities. Currently there are two categories of DART: Reconstructive activities and Processing activities.

Reconstructive activities

These are activities involving a text which the teacher has modified in some manner, and the pupils are expected to reconstruct to its original state. They include:

- word deletion (cloze): pupils are given a copy of the text with significant words missing; pupils should restore the text to its original state with words making complete sense for reasons the pupils should share in discussion;
- paragraph or sentence deletion – the pupils are given a part of the original, perhaps the first and last paragraphs; the activity involves discussing and deciding on what has been missed;
- prediction: the text is divided into sections; at the end of reading each section the pupils discuss what they think is most likely to happen next, from the evidence of their own former reading (of this and other related texts);
- text matching: a text might have certain features removed from it, such as headings or illustrations. Pupils are given these missing elements separately and asked to place them in appropriate positions;
- sequencing: a text is cut up into sections, the sections are given out separately, in any order, and pupils have to rearrange them in order, justifying their reasons.

Processing activities

The processing category of DARTS includes the following activities:

- text marking: pupils are invited to annotate the text in some way, perhaps underlining, using marker pens of different colours to separate sections, placing brackets around related sections, or even circling a section of text and commenting on it at the side;
- representing the text in visual or tabular form: drawing an illustration, to show that the text has been understood, making a time-line, turning facts into tables, columns etc;
- breaking into parts: pupils are asked to divide the text into recognisable sections, and to give reasons for their decisions;
- statements: pupils are supplied with some statements about the text, some true, others not so accurate, possibly summing up its content; pupils have to discuss to establish which they think have a clear relationship with the original;
- genre games: the pupils rewrite a piece of text in one genre into a text in another genre; turning explanations into instructions, turning a story into a drama script;
- question setting: pupils, in small groups, are asked to devise two or three questions about the text on material contained in it, about which they are not clear; they might exchange questions to see if others can answer them, or share them with the teacher;
- drama: aspects of the text are brought alive by pupils working them out in role-play, hot seating, thought tracking, mantle of the expert drama exercises.

These activities all take some preparation and require a clear commitment from the teacher, but they necessitate pupils 'interrogating' and becoming more heavily involved in the text. It is necessary to relate the expectations to the abilities of the pupils, and select texts which pupils can understand. Most of these engagements are collaborative, and encourage pupils to work out meanings in partnership with others.

Layout of texts and textual changes over time

While researching and analysing a great many science text books published during the last forty years I have noticed a number of important changes of which many science teachers remain largely unaware. The problems for readers presented by these publications are not exclusive to science, and some of the following points will apply to books published to support all subjects:

1. Science text books, like most publications for use in schools, have become increasingly visual. Whereas they were once published with pages of dense

writing, with the occasional diagram, often in the form of a line drawing, modern books have at least an equal proportion of pictures, and a few have more picture (and white space) than written text.

2. This layout causes problems for the reader, as the pictures and text are often laid in blocks around the page, and the reader's eye does not know where to begin reading; in a number of books it is difficult to trace the normal left to right across the page reading movements. Pupils need to be 'shown around' some pages.

3. The pictures on the page are not always consistent. A few books will only reproduce photographs, which can assist the reader to understand the point being made, sometimes, but a few pictures seem to have been chosen at random, and only marginally illuminate a learning idea. An increasing number of books are using mixtures of photographs, line drawings (of chemical apparatus, for instance) and cartoon-type drawings – on the same page. These pictures are performing different roles, and often illustrating separate sorts of ideas. Teachers should not assume that the pupils can understand why the pictures have been included, or assume they know what information should be learned from them. The pictures often need teaching, just as much as the words.

4. In an attempt to reduce the amount of written information, many books are adopting an increasingly 'note-like' attitude, with short bursts of print. To help emphasise particular points, the writers and publishers include devices such as underlining words, or printing them in bold type. These embellishments can often be as confusing as they are helpful. On the same page it is not unusual to find abstract nouns, naming the processes (e.g. reproduction, distillation) alongside verbs (e.g. collide, dissolve) and longer noun phrases (e.g. geographical poles, states of matter) without any sort of distinction. Teachers need to point out to pupils some of these small linguistic differences, as they play an important part in the forming of scientific concepts. (This context would be an excellent opportunity to undertake DARTS text-marking activities.)

5. In a further attempt to reach out to pupils, and make the text book style of writing more accessible, some writers actually change their manner of address to the pupils, which can be confusing. An example from one book begins the paragraph:

> All organisms are made from simple building blocks called cells. The chemical reactions which are needed for living and growing take place inside these cells.

and ends it:

> Bigger and more complicated organisms like you and me are made from a variety of cells.

If teachers are using the reading texts in their subject areas as models for acceptable styles of writing, they should be aware that the books themselves are not always consistent.

Many history text books in recent years have been difficult to read in a conventional way, because they are concerned with presenting examples of evidence – pictures, fragments of text – and then suggesting exercises to carry out with that evidence in boxes, randomly placed around the page. Too many history books are still written in an over-metaphoric style, although writers are beginning to take a little more care. All these phrases appeared on one page of a text book, seen in an Oxford middle school classroom in the mid-1990s:

> Henry VIII had three children: Edward, Mary and Elizabeth. All of them wore the English crown..... Her early life was spent under the shadow of the axe..... she too fell out of favour..... She had to use her native wit and intelligence to keep her head above water – and on her shoulders..... Unwittingly, Elizabeth became the centre of Protestants plots.

The writer may have enjoyed these phrases, but they do little to share real information about this reign. What would a not very confident English as an Additional Language pupil make of such material, unmediated?

The real lesson to be learned from the observations made in the previous paragraphs is that teachers should not trust the books they buy into their departments. Publishers are not always aware of the reading difficulties that the books they produce may cause for readers, and some are more concerned with making books look attractive and 'modern' than with assisting learning. Many textbook publishers were unaware, until the National Literacy Strategy was implemented across the country, that their books, or passages within the books, might be considered as different text types or genres. Books should not be placed in front of pupils without teachers having thought about the problems they might cause for the reader. This could possibly be a skill that many teachers are not confident about attempting, but could be improved if a school is aware of the issue and offers INSET sessions where colleagues from different departments could share their own development. Once again, I recommend the using of DARTS techniques, to make the meaning of the texts come alive; perhaps by the teachers too!

Readability

When teachers are reminded that some books used in their lessons might present difficulties for their pupils, they often think it has to do with the inappropriate language levels of those texts. Sometimes this problem has been overlooked by both writer and teacher, but it is not the only barrier to successful reading, as we have already seen. Nevertheless, it is not unusual to find particular passages in books, and even whole books, which make excessive demands on the reader.

There are 'readability' tests available and it would be instructive for departments to submit their texts – published and worksheet materials – to these tests occasionally, to remind themselves of the level of support always necessary to ensure textual material is appropriate. One of the quickest ways of establishing whether pupils can read the book is to ask them, individually, to read a passage out loud, and to count how many problems they encounter with a page. It would be as well to share with the pupils what is taking place, and to invite them to comment on the ways it could be made more relevant to them. Teachers adopting this sort of approach are, anyway, likely to be concerned about the potential difficulties of the text.

The digital divide

An enormous potential problem is currently quietly building up, but will explode on schools during the next few years. As computer and communications technology moves forward, so some groups will be economically and motivationally able to keep up with its development, while others are bound to be left behind. Those pupils who currently have access to computer hardware allowing them to make contact, through the internet, with multiple sources of information, are already at a great distance from their peers. Some pupils are occasionally able to use computers, and they may know something of the interactive nature of information CDs. They may sometimes even have an opportunity to practise that knowledge. For considerable numbers of young people, however, the sorts of new reading skills and knowledges required to deploy the expanding technologies in worthwhile ways are not readily available, and their schools will find it increasingly difficult to help them make up any shortfall.

The research about reading on computer screens is still in its infancy. But there are many different reading contexts possible to identify in which a range of reading practices will be assumed as a necessary prerequisite for learning in just a few years. Ironically, while adopting a warning position, suggesting that our current reading frameworks are inadequate preparation for the immediate future, I am not in a position to identify exactly what young people will require to make satisfactory educational progress. It is simply not possible to predict which technologies will be available to us, except that rather than being computers, they are likely to be made of *computers*. E-mail, internet search-engine language, textual layout and textual interaction will be among the features which will challenge former notions of literacy. No doubt still and moving pictures, and sound, will be used more frequently and naturally alongside printed and spoken text. It is likely that reading and text-making will be more collaborative activities, possibly established in 'workshop' situations. Tweddle *et al.* (1997) state:

> In one very obvious sense we shall, in order to claim to be well educated, have to understand more than we generally do at present about the communicative choices available to us and about what forms as well as what media are most appropriate at a given moment. Our pupils will need to be both craftspersons and artists, well versed in literacy skills at a number of levels.

Young people, indeed all people in an age of true life-long learning, will need to be able to recognise types of text, relationships between text, and make decisions about the appropriate use of text on a scale not yet imagined. Teaching reading in that setting will be a rather broader, less content-led, more culturally aware, personally enhancing set of activities than anything currently known to us. It has to be!

Bibliography

Adams, M. J. (1990) *Beginning to Read: Thinking and Learning about Print.* Cambridge, Massachusetts: MIT Press.

Anderson, R. C., Hiebert, E. H., Scott, J. A. and Wilkinson, I. A. (1985) *Becoming a Nation of Readers: The Report of the Commission on Reading.* Washington DC. US Department of Education.

Barton, G. (1999) 'The state we're in', Book review in *Times Educational Supplement* 22.1.99, 24.

Barton, G. (1992) 'Personal Response to Literature: How Personal is Personal?', in *Use of English* **43,** 2.

Barrs, M. and Pidgeon, S. (1998) *Boys and Reading.* London: CLPE.

Barrs, M. and Thomas, A. (1991) *The Reading Book.* London: CLPE.

Beard, R. (1998) *National Literacy Strategy: Review of Research and other Related Evidence.* London: DfEE.

Bearne, E. (1998) *Making Progress in English.* London: Routledge.

Bisiker, W. and Pidgeon, S. 'A reading tradition', in Barrs, M. and Pidgeon, S. (eds) (1988) *Boys and Reading.* London: CLPE.

Black, P. and Wiliam, D. (1998) *Inside the Black Box.* London: Kings College, London.

Brindley, S. (1994) Introduction in Brindley, S. (ed.) *Teaching English.* London: Routledge, Open University Press.

Browne, A. (1999) 'Windows into Illustration', in *Books for Keeps* No. 118, September 1999.

Cairney, T. H. (1995) *Pathways to Literacy.* London: Cassell.

Calthorp, K. (1971) *Reading Together: An Investigation into the Use of the Class Reader.* London: Heinemann (for NATE).

Chambers, A. (1993) *Tell me: Children, reading and talk.* Stroud: The Thimble Press.

Clipson-Boyles, S. (1995) 'Time Well Spent?', in *Language and Learning*, December.

Collins, F., Hunt, P. and Nunn, J. (1997) *Reading Voices: Young People Discuss their Reading Choices.* London: Northcote House Publishers.

Daly, C. (1999) 'Getting into Books', in *Secondary English Magazine* **3**, 1, 10–12.

Davies, C. (1996) *What is English Teaching?* Buckingham: Open University Press.

Department for Education (1995) *English in the National Curriculum.* London: HMSO.

Department for Education and Employment (1998) *The National Literacy Strategy – Framework for Teaching.* London: DfEE.

Department for Education and Science (1975) *A Language for Life* (The Bullock Report) London: HMSO.

Department of Employment, Education and Training (1992) *Putting Literacy on the Agenda.* Canberra: DEET.

Derewianka, B. (1990) *Exploring How Texts Work.* New South Wales: Primary English Teaching Association.

Dole, J. A., Duffy, G. G., Roehler, L. R. and Pearson, P. D. 'Moving from the old to the new: Research on reading comprehension instruction', in *Review of Educational Research* 61(3), 239–64.

Durkin, D. (1979) 'What classroom observations reveal about reading comprehension instruction', in *Reading Research Quarterly* XIV, 481–537.

Fleming, M. and Stevens, D. (1998) *English Teaching in the Secondary School.* London: David Fulton Publishers.

Griffith, P. (1987) *Literary Theory and English Teaching.* Milton Keynes: Open University Press.

Hall, C. and Coles, M. (1999) *Children's Reading Choices.* London: Routledge.

Harrison, C. (1995) 'The Assessment of Response to Reading: Developing a Post-Modern Perspective', in Goodwyn, A. *English and Ability.* London: David Fulton Publishers.

Harrison, C. and Coles, M. (eds) (1992) *The Reading for Real Handbook.* London: Routledge.

Harrison, C. and Gardner, K. (1977) 'The Place of Reading', in Marland, M. *Language across the Curriculum.* London: Heinemann Educational Books.

Juel, C. (1988) 'Learning to Read and Write: a Longitudinal Study of 54 Children from First through Fourth Grades', in *Journal of Educational Psychology* **80**, 437–47.

Kress, G. (1979) 'Two Kinds of Power: Gunther Kress on Genre', an interview in the *English Magazine* 24, Spring 1991.

Kress, G. (1995) *Writing the Future: English and the Making of a Culture of Innovation.* Sheffield: NATE.

Lewis, M. and Wray, D. (1995) *Developing Children's Non-fiction Writing.* Leamington Spa: Scholastic.

Lewis, M. and Wray, D. (1997) *Writing Frames*. Reading: Reading and Language Information Centre, University of Reading.

Literacy Taskforce (1997) *The Implementation of the National Literacy Strategy*. London: DfEE.

Littlefair, A. (1991) *Reading All Types of Writing*. Buckingham: Open University Press.

Lunzer, E. and Gardner, K. (1979) *The Effective Use of Reading*. London: Heinemann (for the Schools Council).

Lunzer, E. and Gardner, K. (1984) *Learning from the Written Word*. Oxford: Heinemann.

Mawdsley, J.(1990) 'Picture a Book for All Ages', in Wallen, M. (ed.) *Every Picture Tells...* Sheffield: NATE.

Meek, M. (1996) *Information and Book Learning*. Stroud: The Thimble Press.

Millard, E. (1997) *Differently Literate: Boys, Girls and the Schooling of Literacy*. London: Falmer Press.

Peim, N. (1993) *Critical Theory and the English Teacher: Transforming the Subject*. London: Routledge.

Peim, N. (1999) 'A Grammar for the 21st century (2)', in *The Secondary English Magazine* **2**(3) 28–31.

Pemberton, L. and Davidson, N. (1999) *First Steps Literacy Development Continuum*. Oxford: GHPD.

Poulson, L. (1998) *The English Curriculum in Schools*. London: Cassell.

Protherough, R. (1983) *Developing Response to Fiction*. Milton Keynes: The Open University Press.

Protherough, R. (1995) 'What is a Reading Curriculum?', in Protherough, R. and King, P. *The Challenge of English in the National Curriculum*. London: Routledge.

Protherough, R. and Atkinson, J. (1994) 'Shaping the Image of an English Teacher', in Brindley, S (ed.) *Teaching English*. London: Routledge/Open University Press.

QCA English team (1998) *The grammar papers: perspectives on the teaching of grammar in the National Curriculum*. London: QCA.

QCA English team (1999) *Not whether but how: Teaching grammar in English at Key Stages 3 and 4.* London: QCA.

Rees, D. (1994) *First Steps Reading: Developmental Continuum*. Melbourne: Longman.

Reynolds, T. (1995) 'Boys and English: So What's the Problem?', in *English and Media Magazine* **33**, 15–18.

Simons, M. and Richards, C. (1991) 'Two kinds of Power: Gunther Kress on Genre', in *English and Media Magazine* **24**, Spring.

Strang, R. (1967) 'The Nature of Reading', in Melnik, A. and Merritt, J. (eds) (1972) *Reading Today and Tomorrow*. London: The Open University Press.

Traves, P. (1994) 'Reading', in Brindley, S. (ed.) *Teaching English*. London: Routledge/Open University Press.

Tweddle, S., Adams, A., Clarke, S., Scrimshaw, P. and Walton, S. (1997) *English for Tomorrow*. Buckingham: The Open University Press.

Vygotsky, L. (1986) *Thought and Language*. Cambridge, Massachusetts: MIT Press.

Watson, V. (1993) 'Multi-layered Texts and Multi-layered Readers', in Styles, M. and Drummond, M. J. *The Politics of Reading*. Cambridge: University of Cambridge Institute of Education & Homerton College.

Watson, V. (1996) 'Imaginationing *Granpa*: journeying into reading with John Burningham', in Watson, V. and Styles, M. *Talking Pictures*. London: Hodder & Stoughton.

Webster, A., Beveridge, M. and Reed, M. (1996) *Managing the Literacy Curriculum*. London: Routledge.

West, A. (1986) 'The Production of Readers', in *The English Magazine* **17**, 4–9.

Widdowson, H. (1988) 'Appendix 3 – Note of Reservation', in Department of Education and Science *Report of the Committee of Inquiry into the Teaching of English Language*. London: HMSO.

Wilks, J. (1998) 'Reading for Pupils aged 11–14', in Cox, B. (ed.) *Literacy is not Enough*. London/Manchester: Book Trust/Manchester University Press.

Wray, D. and Lewis, M. (1997) *Extending Literacy: children reading and writing non-fiction*. London: Routledge.

Index